# Family Group Conferences in
# Child Welfare

Other titles in the series

*Introduction to Therapeutic Play*
J. Carroll
0-632-04148-X

*Patterns of Adoption*
D. Howe
0-632-04149-8

*Neglected Children: issues and dilemmas*
O. Stevenson
0-632-04146-3

*Young Carers and their Families*
S. Becker, C. Dearden and J. Aldridge
0-632-04966-9

*Child Welfare in the UK*
Edited by O. Stevenson
0-632-04993-6
ISBN: 978-0-6320-4922-6

**Also available from Blackwell Science**

*Child and Family Social Work*
Editor: Professor David Howe
ISSN 1356-7500

*Child and Family Social Work* is a major international journal for all those concerned with the social and personal well-being of children and those who care for them. The Journal publishes original and distinguished contributions on matters of research, theory, policy and practice in the field of social work with children and their families. It aims to give international definition to the discipline and practice of child and family social work.

*Child and Family Social Work* is published quarterly

WORKING TOGETHER FOR CHILDREN,
YOUNG PEOPLE AND THEIR FAMILIES

*SERIES EDITOR:* PROFESSOR OLIVE STEVENSON

# Family Group Conferences in Child Welfare

Peter Marsh

*Reader in Applied Social Studies*
*Department of Sociological Studies,*
*The University of Sheffield*

and

Gill Crow

*Research Fellow & Consultant Clinical Child Psychologist*
*Department of Sociological Studies,*
*The University of Sheffield*

Blackwell
Science

© 1998 by
Blackwell Science Ltd
Editorial Offices:
Osney Mead, Oxford OX2 0EL
25 John Street, London WC1N 2BL
23 Ainslie Place, Edinburgh EH3 6AJ
350 Main Street, Malden
  MA 02148 5018, USA
54 University Street, Carlton
  Victoria 3053, Australia

Other Editorial Offices:

Blackwell Wissenschafts-Verlag GmbH
Kurfürstendamm 57
10707 Berlin, Germany

Blackwell Science KK
MG Kodenmacho Building
7–10 Kodenmacho Nihombashi
Chuo-ku, Tokyo 104, Japan

First published 1998

Set in 10/12 pt Sabon
by DP Photosetting, Aylesbury, Bucks
Printed and bound in Great Britain by
Hartnolls Ltd, Bodmin, Cornwall

The Blackwell Science logo is a trade mark
of Blackwell Science Ltd, registered at the
United Kingdom Trade Marks Registry

DISTRIBUTORS

Marston Book Services Ltd
PO Box 269
Abingdon
Oxon OX14 4YN
(*Orders:*  Tel: 01235 465500
        Fax: 01235 465555)

USA
Blackwell Science, Inc.
Commerce Place
350 Main Street
Malden, MA 02148 5018
(*Orders:*  Tel:  800 759 6102
               617 388 8250
        Fax: 617 388 8255)

Canada
Copp Clark Professional
200 Adelaide Street West, 3rd Floor
Toronto, Ontario M5H 1W7
(*Orders:*  Tel:  416 597-1616
               800 815-9417
        Fax: 416 597-1617)

Australia
Blackwell Science Pty Ltd
54 University Street
Carlton, Victoria 3053
(*Orders:*  Tel: 03 9347 0300
        Fax: 03 9347 5001)

A catalogue record for this title
is available from the British Library

ISBN 0-632-04922-7

Library of Congress
Cataloging-in-Publication Data
Marsh, Peter, 1950–
    Family group conferences in child
welfare/Peter Marsh and Gill Crow.
        p.      cm.— Working together for
children, young people, and their
families
    ISBN 0-632-04922-7 (pbk.)
    1. Family social work.  2. Social
case work with children.  3. Social
case work with youth.  I. Crow, Gill.
II. Title.  III. Series.
HV697.M39   1997
362.71—dc21                    97-26471
                                    CIP

To our families, who loyally forfeited attention
in the course of family research

# Contents

# Foreword
# by Professor Olive Stevenson

This book describes and discusses an important development in child welfare practice in Britain – bringing together members of the wider family network to discuss what should be done to help children and young people in difficulty. The principles underlying such a project are consistent with recent trends, in which we have attempted to redress the balance of power between professionals and the (nuclear) family. These have laid the foundation for the next phase, in which family involvement goes beyond parents.

In so doing, tangible and concrete recognition is given to something of which we are all aware but often do not act upon. Behind the model of the nuclear family, often presented as a tight kind of circle, there lie other influences and forces of great significance to the functioning of the nuclear family. These operate both directly and in terms of actual contact but also in the heads of the adults and children who have deeply held feelings and beliefs about past and present relationships.

The sensible assumption underlying the family group conference is that we should mobilise these influences and forces to help resolve the problems which children and young people have. It is interesting that, in so doing, we have used the experience of Maoris in New Zealand who were accustomed to drawing in the wider family to such situations.

Peter Marsh and Gill Crow offer a very detailed commentary on, and guide to, the issues which arise, based on sound research involving six social service departments. Thus, we now have a good idea which has been tested in practice and can be carefully watched. It is clear that these conferences can be valuable; it is also clear that there are many issues which have to be tackled if they are to be effective. Marsh and Crow have provided an analysis which will be essential reading for those who wish to develop the practice. The idea has excited considerable enthusiasm in practitioners; it is to be hoped that this movement will be more than a passing fashion because it symbolises an important recognition of wider family significance and responsibility. This will be more easily achieved if the circumstances in which this model is particularly useful are clearly identified and the time and resources needed are therefore seen to be well justified.

The energy and efforts of all those involved in the project, including the researchers, give a heartening indication that, despite huge pressures and scarce resources, child welfare practice in this country can be both principled and dynamic.

Olive Stevenson
*Professor Emeritus of Social Work Studies*
*University of Nottingham*

# Preface

Our interest in Family Group Conferences arose, in part, from their early development and the implicit and explicit links between user movements and practitioners. The innovative elements of the model have come from both user and practitioner initiatives, supported by the links between research and practice that have also interested us both separately, in the past. The Conferences have generated international interest, and they are occurring in many different countries, sometimes as part of quite radical legislation. These origins, developments and innovations are not that common in child welfare, and it seemed to us that Family Group Conferences were not an everyday development. They fitted well with many of the child welfare trends of recent years but they were different from most solutions in their origins, and as this book outlines, in their practice.

Our interest was underpinned by the way the Conference model emphasised so strongly some of the foundations of the best child welfare practice, such as the central concern for the child, the focus on the strengths of families rather than their weaknesses, and the emphasis on the child's family as an undeniable part of his or her life.

Bringing the family together to see if they could find solutions to problems that individuals and institutions had difficulties in resolving, seemed to us a development that was well worth exploring. We did so with interest but caution. Anyone involved in the work of the Conferences is bound to find them interesting, just as most of us find families interesting, in their histories, their arguments, their joys and their sorrows. But this interest in the Conferences, especially in the context of high risk child welfare work, should be exercised with care. In our view Family Group Conferences merit serious thought and serious evaluation. That is the intention of this book.

We hope that in the book we have expressed both our interest and our caution. We wanted to help people make informed decisions about Family Group Conferences, to understand some of the theory and background of the Conferences, and to see what the main contribution of Conferences might be to their area of interest. To do this we outline research undertaken over a number of years of experimental work, which describes and analyses the development and outcomes of the model.

The work described in this book is applied social science, and it describes and analyses the efforts of some very able colleagues, and some remarkable children, young people and family members. The intention is that the book will add to our knowledge of good child welfare practice, and that researchers, trainers, practitioners, managers and policy makers will find it directly valuable in their continuing efforts to improve the services that are needed by vulnerable children and their families.

*Peter Marsh* and *Gill Crow*

# Acknowledgements

There are many people whom we should thank for their contributions to the work in this book: the families who showed such courage, all the staff who worked extra hours and went the extra mile and the support from Family Rights Group which provided the foundation of the work. Kate Morris has been an excellent fellow trainer and informed commentator, and the Rough Guide for co-ordinators owes much to her abilities.

Our research colleagues at Sheffield have provided able support. The project managers, and co-ordinators have been splendid colleagues, and although it is invidious to name individuals in this group, Glyn Hughes, Mair Jones, Paul Nixon, Carmel Shepherd and Fiona Wallace have played particularly prominent roles in helping our thinking about Family Group Conferences.

We have welcomed the support from fellow researchers in the UK, and from overseas colleagues, particularly in Portland Oregon, and from Gay Maxwell and Ian Hassall in New Zealand. Many other people, through debate, training sessions, case studies, and research contributions have helped us on our way. We are very grateful to them all.

# Chapter 1

# Introduction:
# Care Services and Families

For many decades the statutory child care service in Britain has been 'observing, questioning, and experimenting to find the right answer for very different individual children and their families' (Younghusband, 1978: p. 37). This book is about exactly that process. It examines the process and outcome of state services for troubled children, and for the families of those children, via a major developmental research project which has established and evaluated the use of Family Group Conferences (Marsh & Crow, 1996).

The background to this research project consists of the changing, questioning and developing child welfare world over the past 25 years. In this period there have been substantial debates and developments affecting both policy and practice, and research and legislative changes have made major contributions to child welfare. The development of the Family Group Conference programme was both a response to the positive opportunities that have been opened up by practice and policy developments and also a reaction to the fact that some problems, particularly as regards substantial family involvement, seem to have been stubbornly prominent over many years.

This chapter discusses the interlinking of the family's consideration of child welfare problems with the professionals' consideration of those problems. It outlines the focus of the research programme, and reviews the way that partnership has become an important part of social work practice with children and families. The important issues of the judgement of seriousness, of enhancing involvement and of gaining agreement are then covered before moving on to outline a way in which the extended family, in a new form of partnership with services, may be involved in debates about these issues. Finally we provide a brief summary of the Family Group Conference approach, and the way that the pilot programme has been developed, evaluated and reported in this book.

## Families, services and child welfare problems

Many children will face welfare problems, ranging from those whose physical environment is very poor, to those whose behaviour is creating social problems, to those who are maltreated by a parent at home. Each day numerous children, and their families, face these difficulties; they find that their welfare is far from ideal. What is likely to happen? In professional language, people will undertake some sort of assessment of these problems, they will come to decisions about them, and they may or may not provide or seek some form of intervention to deal with them. Put another way, there will probably be discussions between a number of family members about this problem, perhaps by those directly involved, perhaps by those witnessing the problems at a greater distance. The individuals who are prepared to be *involved* will see themselves as having some responsibility, and some right, to make these attempts to help. They may argue about that right, and as a result play a greater or lesser role. They will probably come to some understanding, explicit or implicit, amongst themselves as to what is needed. Some sorts of actions will probably be taken. For the vast majority of children, even in particularly bad circumstances, the people doing this 'assessment, decision-making and intervention' will be family members.

The young person may take these actions, seeing a need to do something to improve things for her- or himself. A parent, probably a mother, as mothers carry by far the major burden of family care, may seek to change the child's actions for the better. A grandparent may seek to cajole their offspring, or possibly spend some time caring directly for their grandchild. Step-family may well be actively involved. It is also quite possible that some people will be prepared to act *as if family*, perhaps those who have some honorary status, the people referred to by children and their parents as 'uncle this' or 'aunty that' despite the fact that they have no direct family connection, or the close friend who undertakes many family-like actions. These people may offer advice, welcomed or not, and may engage in the process of debate and consequent action to try and improve the welfare of the child. Every day of every week hundreds of thousands of people undertake *child welfare work*.

Of course the child welfare problems may spill out beyond the family, and involve professionals. Even then it will probably not come to a *child welfare professional* such as a social worker. If the problem does have effects beyond the family it is most likely to be felt in a more universal service for children, within health or, perhaps predominantly, within schools. If this does occur, then the private problem, albeit shared amongst family, enters a more public arena. A school teacher, for example, may raise worries about school performance with a young person or parent, and suggest that the school problems may interlink in some way with home problems. This may trigger other professionals to take an interest.

Usually slowly, and sometimes quite fast, there comes into being a public social problem for this child or young person.

## Support, networks, families and services

Once there is a public social problem, how do the services and families interact? Who is going to be involved, who sees whom, who does what? Up to now we have been focusing on the family *as* a social service, now there is an additional element of the family *dealing with* a social service.

We shall return to the family as a social service in the next chapter, when we consider the ways in which the individuals within the family network may engage, or not, to support the welfare of the child. At this point we will consider the interaction of the family with the professionals. The *family* comprises a network of individuals, but as we shall see the literature regarding the way that family networks respond to child welfare services is rather thin. This is in some distinction to the more developed work on family networks and the care of older people in the community (see for example, Qureshi & Walker, 1989; Wenger, 1984, 1994). While the *idea* of family support is strong in the literature and ethos of child welfare, it is still the case that much of the available empirical research focuses on professional services in conjunction with individuals rather than a network.

Child welfare research, at least that part of it which focuses on the higher risk groups in contact with social workers, has usually concentrated on worker–user exchanges involving only the immediate recipients of that exchange. Child welfare studies have generally looked at the immediate user of the service, in conjunction with outcomes for the child concerned, and interpreted any network events via the commentary of that user. How do networks respond before professional involvement, what happens within the wider family, how are family roles negotiated and what are children's own networks? ... these questions, if they are asked, are usually answered via the main user, who will nearly always be the main carer of the child.

*Family* can come to mean main carer(s) of the child: the importance of the wider family often appears to be missed. As a recent government overview of research (Department of Health, 1995a: p. 49) has stated

> 'Myopia hindered discussion about a child's "family". The common preoccupation was with the nuclear aspect, which more often than not consisted of a single female parent or involved step-parents, situations where there were frequently specific problems, irrespective of any abuse. On the other hand, the significance of wider patterns of kinship and other sources of emotional support was often overlooked.'

Greater attention to the interaction of family support and service support, and to considering family as more than the household, or the nuclear family, is clearly of importance in the future development of child welfare services.

*The families in the study*

This book is about the inter-relationship of child welfare services and the family, in situations where there are substantial problems regarding the welfare of a child or young person. It is inevitably set in the context of a long-standing and wider debate about the role of the state and the family in the general upbringing of children (see Moroney, 1976). What role should the state play, for example, in educating children or providing a framework of moral values? These are important debates, touching at the heart of the way that British children's welfare, understood in its widest sense, should be supported and enhanced in late twentieth century industrialised society. It can spread out into wide-ranging political debates about the role of private and public provision, and into moral and spiritual debates about values and the family. To some extent we must touch on these, and where needed we shall do so, but the focus of this book is at a more detailed level than these broad-brush issues.

This book is about the group of children who are in households at the margins of coping, and where they and their parents have some contact with social services departments. They are 'children in need' in the language of the Children Act 1989. It is primarily about a subdivision of this group: those where there is some argument about that level of need, and where for one reason or another it seems that the family is not able, in reasonably straightforward discussion with social services or others, to meet the reasonable needs of their children and to safeguard their welfare. It is, in short, about the group of children which social workers spend much of their time worrying about, as well as possibly a sprinkling of those that they should spend more time worrying about.

But it is, of course, not just social workers who will do the worrying. Even within the higher risk groups that concern us here, the great majority of *child welfare work* is done by families. As a recent review of child protection investigation has pointed out (Gibbons *et al.*, 1995) over 90% of the children, within the 160 000 referred for child protection enquiries each year, remain at home throughout the enquiry period. Families discuss, decide, act, react and provide day-to-day care throughout this process.

Good services are needed to support families at these difficult times. There are sound arguments to suggest that they should be available before these times, and there is some evidence that preventive services will have an impact in helping families where there are troubled or troubling children (Gibbons, 1990, 1992; Utting *et al.*, 1993).

The three separate tiers of services suggested by Utting *et al.* (1993: p. 28) in connection with children who are in trouble with the justice system all have their role to play in connection with child welfare problems more generally. The first tier comprises universal support services which could be made available to every family, the second provides neighbourhood services which are suitably targeted, for example on socially disadvantaged areas, and the third consists of family preservation services for individual families of children who risk abuse or whose behaviour is seriously disturbed. The study that we report here concentrates on the third level, and concerns the families and children who are going to come into contact with these services.

This group comprises, of course, a small minority of children and, as the typology above suggests, a minority of those in need of services. The children covered by the research described in this study comprise those who are involved in the child protection system or the care system, or who are perhaps on the fringes of each. It concerns children who come to the attention of social services. Some idea of the children under consideration can be seen in Fig. 1.1. These children absorb a great deal of social services' time, a large proportion of social services' budgets, and they experience, and cause, much distress. They form the group examined in this study.

## Partnership between services and families

Over recent years there has come to be something of a consensus regarding the overall way that services and the family should interact for this group of children. In the past a prominent element of the services for this group was to provide professional care as a substitute for family care, an approach based in part on a *rescue* model of services. But in fits and starts since the Children and Young Persons Act 1963 there has been a growing consensus that the best model of service is some form of partnership between professional and user, supporting the care of children within their own family and maintaining very strong family links when this proves impossible (Packman, 1993). We have referred to the model of work, in an earlier study, as one of *assisted parenting*, (Fisher *et al.*, 1986: p. 142). The focus of services is on supporting the difficult task of parenting, maybe at times providing brief or lengthy care away from home in order to do so, but providing help that will enhance the ways that families provide parenting for their children. Although it is clearly more difficult where children are in need of child protection services, there is no doubt that the approach can extend to these children as well, albeit with some limitations and extra care (see for example the *The Challenge of Partnership in Child Protection: Practice Guide* from the Social Services Inspectorate, 1995).

The partnership can be developed via family support services as described by Gibbons and her colleagues (Gibbons, 1992) and in the *tougher* end of the work, with families using the care system (Marsh & Triseliotis, 1996). It has been found to produce good results in a wide range of circumstances (Marsh & Fisher, 1992; DeChillo *et al.*, 1994; Department of Health, 1995a; Thoburn *et al.*, 1995). But it is clearly

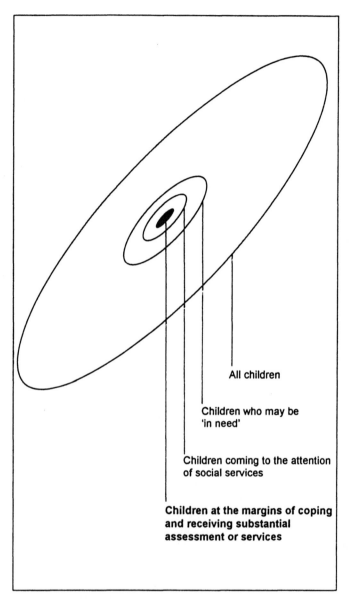

All children

Children who may be
'in need'

Children coming to the attention
of social services

**Children at the margins of coping
and receiving substantial
assessment or services**

**Fig. 1.1**  The children in the study.

difficult to do well, and there are a number of important areas that need
careful consideration when this approach is developed.

*Social workers and their partners*

Who should social workers be in partnership with? What areas should
the partnership cover? These questions and many others, for example

about control and power within the partnership, will concern social workers from the earliest stages. Partners, and partnerships, of course come in all shapes and sizes. In different situations different partners will, for example, have quite different amounts of power, derived from different areas such as status, family history, law and so on. Partnership is not about equality. Partnership's hallmark should be diversity, but within a common frame of principles. These have been well expressed in the training pack for partnership produced to help implement the Children Act. This suggested that:

> 'The essence of partnership is sharing. It is marked by respect for one another, role divisions, rights to information, accountability, competence and value accorded to individual input. In short, each partner is seen as having something to contribute, power is shared, decisions are made jointly, and roles are not only respected but are also backed by legal and moral rights.'

> (Tunnard, 1991a: p. 1)

Sharing is not an easy task. There is continual scope for argument over each and every aspect of a partnership. The process of partnership must be one of debate, one of negotiation.

Three key areas are likely to feature prominently in the partnership debates, and will be more or less heated depending on the different circumstances of each case: the nature of the child welfare problem, who should be involved and how much compulsion is required of whom. Before we move on to consider these, it is important to remember that they will be, to a greater or lesser extent, negotiated *within* families, as well as between families and professionals. There will be times when the negotiation will have to take place within formal rules under the law, and many others when it will be far more informal.

### Negotiation

Partnership is in part a process and its essence may lie in repeated attempts, at many different stages of the work, to obtain agreement between family and professionals regarding both purpose and action. For example, professionals will carry out assessments, concerning 'what has happened to this child, and what are the likely effects on this child?', but that information may be open to a variety of interpretations (see for example the debates between family members and social workers reported in Thoburn *et al.* 1995: pp. 52–53). In this case, and throughout partnership-based work, there will be negotiation. The negotiation is likely to be about very serious issues, and for some families involvement in it is a traumatic and difficult affair, irrespective of outcome (see for example, Cleaver & Freeman, 1995; Farmer & Owen, 1995). There should be no doubt of the professional skill needed to undertake effective negotiation in these circumstances.

Once there is some shared ground regarding problems and needs, then negotiation will move on to the details of solutions. Of course there may be times when negotiation will be too slow, or is getting nowhere, and where social workers must act quickly to protect children. There will be some cases where partnership is slim or non-existent because of the complete unwillingness of family members to negotiate. But *total* breakdown of relationships should be very uncommon, and even in apparently unpromising situations elements of partnership may well be feasible, although probably dependent on reasonably high levels of worker skill (Marsh & Fisher, 1992; Thoburn *et al.*, 1995). The idea of partnership as the core of the inter-relationship of services and families in difficult child welfare areas acknowledges that there are, at the margins, limitations to the establishment of these partnerships.

The importance of high levels of skills also imposes some limits. Partnership ideas are endorsed by research, and to some degree in the aspirations of social workers, but they may sit uncomfortably with the image that social workers hold of social work as an activity, and hence the skills they develop and value. Jordan (1987), for example, argues that images of being advocates or counsellors are prominent within social work, and these may involve elements of work that do not sit that comfortably with the needs of negotiation. There is some evidence that social work training may have limited material on partnership (Jackson & Morris, 1994) and indeed that it may not emphasise the relevant research (Marsh & Triseliotis, 1996).

The achievement of partnership is unlikely to be a straightforward affair. Finding ways to advance partnership-based work needs, as we have suggested, to engage better with the family-wide debates that accompany professional intervention and to provide more recognition of the network of extended family. The debates will be about the scale and level of the child welfare problem, about who is generating the problem and who is and should be solving it. They will be about the need for compulsion in dealing with the problem. In short they will involve questions about seriousness, involvement and voluntariness. We shall cover each of these issues in turn.

## Deciding *seriousness*

How much attention should we devote to *this* child welfare problem? Professionals, and family members, must judge *seriousness* as they decide whether or not they should do something on behalf of children, and they assess how rapidly they should act to safeguard children's welfare.

The professional judgement will be within the frame of the Children Act 1989 and its definitions of seriousness, which require professionals to establish whether or not a child is suffering or is likely to suffer 'significant harm' (Adcock *et al.*, 1991). The judgement must include comparisons with what could reasonably be expected of a similar child, and whether or not the significant harm is attributable to current care. These surely are very similar questions to those that must go through many parents' and other family members' minds as they consider the *seriousness* of problems affecting the welfare of a child.

Professional judgements are forged in the context of the family ones. We know for example that problems often build up over some considerable time, and that there is a cumulative effect on parents with requests to social services being triggered by a *last straw* (Fisher *et al.*, 1986: p. 43). The impact of a current crisis may only really be understood against its backdrop, and *small* problems may need the explanation of their substantial pedigree.

The context of events may well be a key factor in their impact on children. Acts of bad treatment of children may have very different effects in different contexts (Rutter & Smith, 1995). How difficult is it to understand these contexts in the current judgements about seriousness? The detail that matters so much is often hard to collect, and the feeling of taking one photographic still shot from the continuing film of family life must be an experience common to many professional discussions of family circumstances and backgrounds. Finding ways to introduce the maximum amount of information into the debates is important for children's welfare, as has been recognised in the policy of involving parents directly in child protection conferences.

Child welfare problems involve complex judgements and debates about seriousness, intertwined with judgements about the ways that services will, could or should react to the revelation of concerns. The judgements involve a set of negotiations between those people with knowledge and an interest in the child, including family members, and of course the child or young person themself. They are about a series of thresholds which problems need to reach to trigger different sorts of actions. These will be different in different family cultures. They will be different for the carer of the child as compared with, for example, the child's aunt, and they can be informed by, but not fully defined by, scientific evidence as to what is harmful for children. How can we provide a suitable forum for these debates which will ensure that a *bottom line* is defined for the protection of children, but which will recognise that family members have a key role to play within the defining of problems and the working out of responses to them? One avenue has been the development of parental participation in child protection conferences, but are there other models which might be worth exploring alongside this one and which could accommodate the wider family? Can we add the extended family knowledge to the debate about seriousness?

## Engaging in the debate

Who should be involved with this debate? For the complex and serious issues under consideration here there is little doubt that wide involvement is, in principle, a good thing. It has long been recognised that a number of professional views are more likely to provide a sound judgement about the care of a child, and that more than one service may be needed to help with that care. The debate about involvement has generally focused on the need for multiprofessional involvement. When it has concerned families it has generally focused on those immediately caring for the child, and under the Children Act 1989, those with *parental responsibility*. It has also focused on parental contribution to formal meetings, principally child protection conferences or child care reviews, or the issues concerned in working with parents in partnership.

It is clear that work needs to continue on multiprofessional engagement. For example, on the professional side while there are substantial numbers of professionals attending child protection conferences (Gibbons *et al.*, 1995) it appears that communication and joint working between them outside of the formal child protection meeting is all too often rather poor (Audit Commission, 1994). As Hallett (1995) comments there is a rise and fall in interagency cooperation, with much more of it occurring at the initial stages of professional child welfare intervention, and much less of it beyond this. Professional cooperation is a problem that clearly merits much more work, but this should not obscure the need to make sure that involvement of family members is also enhanced.

In current social work practice there is much greater involvement of users in general, and both the number of people and the depth of their involvement has increased over recent years. The idea of partnership in social work assessment, decision-making and services has emphasised the importance of this. However it is not surprising, given their central role in caring for children, that mothers are the main focus of much of child welfare work, with resident fathers or step-fathers trailing a fair distance behind them, and with other members of the family much less likely to be involved. This is true in the wider realm of child care problems (Fisher *et al.*, 1986) and in the more limited area of child protection (Thoburn *et al.*, 1995). The complexity of family structure, an issue we will return to, also appears somewhat unrecognised in social work practice, for example the need to work more in partnership with step-parents (Loughran & Riches, 1996). In general it seems likely that active involvement with social services on child welfare problems is still relatively limited within families, and rarely extends much beyond the nuclear family. There is substantial scope for greater involvement of the extended family and it may well pay dividends (Thoburn *et al.*, 1995: p. 64).

Achieving this involvement means recognition of the way that family roles and responsibilities develop and evolve over time (see Finch & Mason, 1993) and the way that they may change over different issues. Many people rely heavily on family, as we shall see in the next chapter, but they may also go out of their way to avoid such reliance. Support is certainly not directly predictable on the basis of kin relationships (Finch & Mason, 1993: p. 164). Responsibilities are created and developed by and within family networks (Allan, 1996: pp. 67–83), but they do not form absolute rights. The complex picture about seriousness is mirrored by an equally complex one regarding the different roles and responsibilities of family members. The picture is different for each family in each different circumstance. Can we find ways to extend family involvement that reflect the reality of varying and different family patterns and individual responses to them?

## Gaining agreement

The concerns about child welfare are unlikely to arise entirely in an atmosphere of agreement. Some parties are likely to be reluctant participants. If problems are judged to be serious, and if carers appear unwilling to accept this judgement, then another debate will take place, around the need for some sort of compulsion to force attention on the problems and enhance the welfare of the child. There is likely to be a complex mix of genuine agreement and involuntary acquiescence whenever family members or professionals come to a conclusion about welfare problems. Almost certainly there will be some elements of the problems that are agreed by nearly everyone, and then different shades of agreement beyond this. The same will be true of solutions, with some parties wholeheartedly endorsing them, and others only going along with them because of pressure of one sort or another.

At its sharpest the difficulty of gaining agreement will necessitate decisions about compulsion via courts. Having a court order does not automatically mean that the individuals concerned are reluctant to engage in the work, for example family members may suggest that court orders are effectively immaterial, that it is a family decision for a young person to enter the care system even when it actually came about as a result of a court order (Fisher *et al.*, 1986: p. 37). From the perspective of the young person it may often feel as if things are always done to them, and that everything is compulsory. However, many young people will appreciate that it may be mostly their behaviour that is leading to problems, whatever the origins of that behaviour, or that it may be mostly the behaviour of others, in the form, for example, of lack of care. Jean Packman suggested that the child welfare cases that they studied could be divided up into three groups – the victims, the villains and the volunteered (Packman, 1986). The victims were predominantly those who suffered some form of deprivation at the hands of others, while the villains were those who were developing problems where their own behaviour was prominent. The volunteered occupied some middle ground where situational issues, such as parents' health, seemed dominant. Young people, in different ways at different ages, need to understand their own circumstances and the arguments going on around them if they are to be properly involved in the decisions about their own futures. They may need to debate, or even perhaps negotiate, whether or not they are victim, villain or volunteered, and they will need to do this, at least in part, with their own families.

Exactly as with the previous two areas there are complex negotiations, which will look very different from case to case. It is clear, and in many respects self-evident, that feeling forced to accept judgements is likely to be the least satisfactory from the family's point of view (Department of Health, 1995b; Packman, 1986). Achieving some agreement, achieving some voluntariness, is very important.

Some agreement is most likely to maximise the chances of those most closely involved with the child taking the necessary actions to promote that child's welfare. Put crudely you are far more likely to carry out actions if you feel some measure of agreement with them. That agreement, for example about suitable standards of child care, may of course be given under some pressure and in that circumstance it is most likely to be maintained if there is continuing pressure. Family members may be well placed to apply such pressure.

Professionals need to seek ways to encourage genuine debate and to try to establish common ground with family members. In so far as the agreement is given under some pressure concerning child care standards there needs to be a likelihood of continuing pressure to avoid retrenchment. Can we produce ways that will maximise the chance of agreement and encourage continued adherence to that agreement?

## Providing a framework for partnership with extended family

The questions outlined above provide a possible framework within which the negotiations of partnership-based social work may take place. Such negotiations should provide good information in order to consider seriousness, should engage relevant family members and should seek to achieve agreement. These principles have lain behind child welfare policy development in recent years, but there is merit in continuing to advance them to build a deeper sense of partnership with greater involvement of the extended family.

## Developing services

Overall there has undoubtedly been progress in these areas over the past decades. The values underpinning them, as we have discussed, are at the heart of the Children Act 1989; practice and policy are evolving along these directions. However as we have seen, and will continue to see, throughout all of this progress there continues to be a lack of attention to the extended family. There are significant opportunities for the extended family to help more with the welfare of troubled children. As Bullock and his colleagues have commented:

'for the great majority of children in care, family members are the most important resources available to social workers, for it is parents, grand-parents, siblings and wider family who are likely to provide continuing and unconditional support. It may be true that some children in care reluctantly go back to relatives because they have nobody else. Nevertheless whether professionals like it or not, almost all children in care will eventually be restored to their family and our perspectives and interventions need to accommodate that fact.'

(Bullock *et al.*, 1993: p. 67)

The extended family has continued as a relatively neglected area throughout the positive developments of the past decades, and providing ways to increase the involvement of family members is an important problem to be addressed (Friesen & Koroloff, 1990). Greater involvement should improve the information available to consider seriousness. It should increase the availability of those who may support the child or young person and, if agreement can be reached, provide additional support for the continuing enactment of any child welfare plan that is put into place. The twin aims of greater partnership and the greater involvement of the extended family within that partnership are important to the continuing development of child welfare practice.

## Exhortation, action and evaluation

Suggesting the value of a particular course of action is often, of course, much easier than actually doing it. The promotion of partnership as a practice base within child welfare indicates this general principle; workers have struggled to put *good intentions* into practice (Pugh & De'Ath, 1989: pp. 15–17; Marsh & Fisher, 1992). If there is to be a serious attempt to involve extended family to a greater degree, then there needs to be practical ways to do so, and the practice needs to address the questions that were outlined earlier regarding seriousness, engagement and gaining agreement. Given the difficulty of implementation it would also seem sensible to proceed by pilots and to make sure that those pilots are evaluated.

These were the principles underlying the developmental research that is described here. An interest in increasing partnership and the involvement of the extended family led to an interest in a new model of practice, called Family Group Conferences, that seemed to hold promise for converting exhortation into reality. It was developed and evaluated within a pilot programme within England and Wales. This book covers the story of that programme.

## The Family Group Conference programme

Based on developments in New Zealand and elsewhere the idea of a Family Group Conference as a relevant way to involve extended family and establish a new form of partnership started to grow in the UK in the early 1990s (the origins of the Conferences and an outline of the key dimensions of them are given in Chapter 3). They appeared to provide an arena for consideration of the questions outlined earlier via substantially greater involvement of extended family. Would this prove a practical and effective way to take forward the issues raised?

### *Family Group Conferences*

The Conferences are a meeting of extended family and relevant professionals to consider the welfare of a child, and to decide if possible on a suitable course of action. They are conducted in such a way that the family can engage in quite detailed negotiation both with professionals and amongst its own members. There is a new job of co-ordinator required to make sure that the Conference is conducted well. Preparation of all parties beforehand is very important, and the meeting itself comprises three main stages: the giving of information by professionals and family members, private family discussion and finally the development, if possible, of a plan agreed by all parties.

#### *The key participants*

The Conferences are convened by a co-ordinator who has specific responsibilities for this task. Although paid by social services, he or she is not directly responsible for services or assessment in connection with the family. Their work is to make sure that all relevant people attend the Conference, and that the Conference runs well through its different stages. They should also play a role in monitoring the outcomes of Conferences, including, if necessary, reconvening them.

#### *The conference itself*

Although, as we shall see, the work before and after the actual meeting is extremely important, the Conference is the heart of the process outlined here. This consists of a meeting of all family members with those professionals who have specific information to give about the problems under discussion. Family membership is defined broadly to include the full range of relatives of the child, and those who act in a family-like manner, such as honorary aunts or uncles. The family members will therefore always include members of the extended family as well as parents. Children will nearly always attend, and older children will often be very active participants. If appropriate the co-ordinator may allow, encourage or even require that supporters or advocates for some family members also attend.

Family members and honorary family members are therefore informed and invited, and relevant information is gathered together about the child. The meeting then takes place at a time and place that suits the family best. It has three key stages (Fig. 1.2).

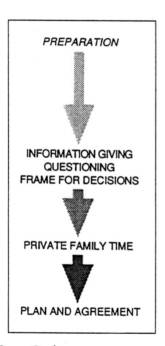

**Fig. 1.2** The Family Group Conference.

- Stage 1: full information is given to the family, and discussed, concerning the problems as seen by professionals.
- Stage 2: is private family time, without professionals, to consider the information, to consider what should be done and what support from family or services might be needed
- Stage 3: is a discussion of the decisions, and an attempt to outline a clear plan which will protect and care for the child and that is agreeable to professionals and all family members.

If no plan can be agreed a repeat Conference may be arranged, or the case will be taken to court by the professionals.

### Process and outcome

The Conference follows a standard and organised agenda, but the process should be substantially affected by family requests (for example the Conference may take place in a family home or on neutral territory, or it may be in an evening and it may follow some of the traditions of the particular family, for example a welcome to all members from a respected grandparent).

In summary, the Conference provides a forum in which plans are developed by the family in the light of the professional and their own information, and they are then negotiated in detail with the professionals before being finalised. If there is no agreement within the family, or if the professionals and family cannot agree in the third stage, then another meeting can be called, or the issue can go to a court for resolution. In practice agreement is nearly always reached.

## Setting it up

While there were good indications from New Zealand and elsewhere that the Conferences could be very successful, there were bound to be problems in the implementation of a model that involved an innovative approach in a complex area (as was also found in New Zealand, see for example Mason *et al.*, 1992). The incorporation of some of the ideas into part of the Department of Health training programme for implementing the Children Act 1989 (Tunnard, 1991b) provided some experience of the way that the model would be received. The response to the training session that featured the Conference was one of great interest but also intense debate. It was clear that implementation would need to be considered very carefully (we return to this issue in Chapters 3 and 4).

In the light of the apparent relevance of the model, and the interest in it, the Family Rights Group, the voluntary organisation that had been commissioned to provide the Children Act 1989 training pack, supported a number of training events specifically on Family Group Conferences.

## The social services involved

Between early 1994 and 1996, eight courses involving 155 staff from 46 social services departments and 25 other agencies were run at Family Rights Group. As a result of these courses a number of social services expressed interest in piloting Family Group Conferences, and a group of six eventually emerged who were prepared to try the model as part of a co-ordinated pilot programme. In the course of further development two of the group dropped out. The selection of this pilot group was in part serendipitous, but there was some element of selective encouragement in order to ensure that there was a range of different departments, spanning city and county, and covering different areas of the child welfare field. Right from the start it was made clear that the work would need to be accompanied by research, and all members of the pilot programme agreed to provide some local evaluation and to contribute to a national research study.

Enthusiasm, rather than guaranteed finance, was the main ingredient of the early days of this group, but all the projects had, or gathered, management backing. In time all of them, with the exception of Hereford and Worcester, obtained agreement for the recruitment of co-ordinators, but there have been very different levels of financial support available for all aspects of the work. A quick pen picture of each of the departments is provided below, and more detail about the implementation in different departments is given in Chapter 4.

### Wandsworth

This London inner city social services department covers a total population of around a quarter of a million in a compact area. It has the usual range of urban problems. The project was initiated by social work practitioners, with some active management support but very little in the way of extra resources for development or co-ordinator costs. Only recently has there been a funded manager for the project.

### Hereford and Worcester

This county social services department covers a population of around three quarters of a million, in a mixed urban and rural area. One staff member developed the work as part of a planning brief, and work was predominantly carried out within three teams using the staff member as co-ordinator. To some degree the work built on, and has been integrated into, existing ways of working in the area.

### Winchester

The Winchester child and families team covers the relatively affluent small town and its surrounding rural area. The project was initiated by practitioners, and received limited but growing levels of financial support, and there is now a full-time project manager.

### Gwynedd

The project covers the town of Caernarfon in North Wales, with a population of around 50 000, many of whom speak Welsh as their first language. The work was initiated by senior management and had some additional resources devoted to it, which have continued in the form of a contractual link with a voluntary agency.

The research that is reported in this book covers these four projects, although at the outset there were two more: Leamington Spa, which was going to concentrate primarily on the local Asian community, and St Basils, in Birmingham, which was going to concentrate on young homeless people. For a variety of reasons, primarily about staff departures or lack of staff time, these two projects did not produce Conferences as part of this study.

The evaluation programme has now moved on to include two additional departments with specific developments associated with each of them. Haringey social services is testing the model intensively within child protection alone, and focusing on a large client group whose heritage is not from the UK. In Wiltshire the model is being implemented in a broad-based initiative combining education, health and social services. In both of these departments, and also in Wandsworth and Hampshire, it is now intended that the model moves beyond a pilot phase to be a part of mainstream practice.

As the programme gathered speed many more social departments expressed interest in carrying out Family Group Conferences and they have now occurred in many places and settings. Some departments have probably carried out Family Group Conferences more in name than in reality, an issue we will return to in Chapter 9, while others have contributed ideas and started to develop research which should continue to inform the development of the model. Internationally there has been very wide interest in the work, of course in New Zealand, but also in Australia, the United States, Canada, Israel, South Africa and Sweden (for a discussion of some of this work see Chapter 5). Clearly the Conferences are seen as having wide potential relevance.

## Data gathered and local studies

The research reported here covers 80 Family Group Conferences in England and Wales, which involved 99 children from 69 families. Co-ordinators provided detailed data describing each Conference. Follow-up data, some 12 months later, were obtained from co-ordinators and from social workers (for details see Crow & Marsh, 1997). Interviews were carried out with 64 of the social workers from the teams involved, including at least half of the membership of each team in the project. The 18 co-ordinators involved were also interviewed as were 15 other professionals. There were specific local studies in each of the four sites, and family views were gathered from three of the projects by these local research studies.

## The programme and this book

The work reported here is based on the programme and research described above. In the next chapter we outline some of the issues regarding extended families in the context of the child welfare focus of the study. In ensuing chapters we cover the details of the Family Group Conference process itself, the experience of implementation and also international developments and research. Although the focus is on child welfare, there is some material on the role of Family Group Conferences in youth justice where there have been major international developments.

We describe the Conferences from the point of view of those implementing them, trainers, co-ordinators and family members. In doing this the outline of the Conference itself is slowly filled in chapter by chapter. We have already provided a brief version above, and there is substantial detail in Chapter 3, including a Rough Guide to co-ordinating conferences. Implementation issues are covered in Chapter 4, and there is more about the Conference process in Chapters 6 and 7. In Chapter 8 we cover the outcomes of the Conferences, before ending on a consideration of the next stages for this innovation in child welfare.

## Conclusions

In this chapter we have examined the way that services, and research, in child welfare have tended to emphasise the nuclear family and to provide relatively little attention to the extended family. The newly developed partnership approach in social work has not been very successful in extending the concept of partner beyond the immediate carers of the child or young person. The development of this approach will involve both the extension of the idea of partnership and finding new ways to enhance negotiation throughout social work practice.

There is a need to add a new dimension to each of three crucial areas in social services' child welfare considerations. When examining the seriousness of situations there is a need for more voices to be heard from a wider range of family members. As regards engaging the family in the debate it needs to be recognised that families are diverse in shape and form, and this diversity needs somehow to be reflected in the models of involvement. Finally there is a need for practice which will make it most likely that voluntary, rather than compulsory, arrangements are made – a difficult enough task with a small number of parties, but even more daunting if the extended family is to be more involved.

The idea of the Family Group Conference as one approach to these issues has been developing in the UK from the early 1990s. The pilot programme that established some of the first Conferences, and that has developed and evaluated them for some 5 years, is the focus of this book. The model has been developed within child welfare and gives voice to a wide number of family members including extended family; it features negotiation throughout and it clearly has merit for tackling some of the issues outlined above. Before we cover more detail of that model, we will turn next to consider some of the roles played by family in the life and welfare of children.

# Chapter 2

# Families and Child Welfare

Problems of children's welfare are inextricably intertwined with the problems of their families. We have argued that there is a need to provide a forum for negotiation between professionals and families, and that wider family involvement in that forum would be welcome. But what, in modern Britain, is the *wider family*, and what role might it play in children's welfare?

This chapter outlines the practical nature of families in modern Britain, and some of their inter-relationships with social services in child welfare. It outlines the way that family is an important source of identity and meaning. It argues that family and kinship are a substantial and continuing practical and psychological force in people's lives. Good child welfare services need to pay close attention to the extended family network.

## *Families* in the UK

Any discussion of *extended* family has to take place in the context of studies, statistics and discussion documents that focus very strongly on the *nuclear* family. There is in general 'a shortage of data relating to the part which grandparents, brothers, sisters, uncles, aunts, and cousins play in children's lives' (Utting, 1995: pp. 28–29). The available research on kinship and its social consequences predominantly dates from the 1950s and 1960s, and as one influential commentator has noted,

> 'the character of kinship bonds has become even more complex as a consequence of the higher incidence in contemporary society of cohabitation, divorce and remarriage. Yet unfortunately our knowledge of kinship in Britain has not developed in response to these changes.'

> (Allan, 1996: p. 35)

Any debates that draw on research will, in common with the social services' issues that we raised in the previous chapter, nearly always be based on considering the family as meaning a *household*.

The fact that statistics are normally gathered on the basis of household reinforces this problem. It means that many presentations of *family* equate with those who are living under one roof. Indeed it might be more realistic to replace the phrase 'children and their families' in many publications with the phrase 'children and their immediate carers'. For material that is explicitly about child care there is a further subdivision that is quite likely to occur, as fathers, with a relatively low profile in caring, seem to drop out of the picture altogether. It is difficult to gather good material for the family policy debate that does not revolve around mothers and their children in the same household.

For many purposes the focus on household may be satisfactory – although the focus on mothers may be more generally problematic, reinforcing pressures on women, and allowing men to be excluded, or exclude themselves, from many child welfare issues. However when the debate is about the family as a social service, the reality of multiple family figures in a child's life needs particular consideration, both from practical and psychological points of view. A full picture of what family consists of, and what family means, needs to be drawn, rather than the more limited one that features in many reports and debates.

## The current picture

There are over 12 million children and young people aged 16 or under in the UK, and around 10 million of these children are in England. This is out of an overall population of the United Kingdom that was, in 1995, around 58 million people. Therefore around one in five of this population was aged under 16 (Office for National Statistics, 1997).

The proportion of children under 16 is substantially different for different ethnic groups. The 20% for white heads of households increases to 30% for Indian heads of household up to 47% for Bangladeshi heritage families (Central Statistical Office, 1994: p. 8). In total just under a million of the young people aged under 16 come from ethnic minority groups.

Around one third of households with children have three or more children present, and nearly half have two (Central Statistical Office, 1994). In modern Britain, in general, people live in comparatively small households: 92% of households consist of four people or less, although the average mean household size of 2.44 hides quite large variations between different ethnic groups, with, for example, households with an Indian head of household having a mean average size of 3.63 people (NCH Action for Children, 1996: p. 27).

Few children live apart from one or other parent; for example in 1991 there were under 40 000 children in 'communal establishments' outside of education, alongside some 60 000 who were in 'educational establishments', and who were predominantly boarding school pupils (Central Statistical Office, 1994: p. 13).

There is a wide diversity of childhood experience of family life in the

UK, varying from children sharing lives with many brothers and sisters, to being an only child, and from having many nieces and nephews to having very few.

The variation in children's sibling and peer experiences extends to the adults present in their lives, although the norm for the great majority of children (80%) is to live in a household with two adults present, and where over three quarters of these couples will be married (NCH Action for Children, 1996). For a substantial minority however, and one that has grown greatly in recent decades, their household will be a single parent, or if it is two adults they will not be married (Utting, 1995: p. 17).

If there are two adults in the household then they may well not be the natural parents, as around 175 000 children are in families which experience separation each year. There are therefore substantial changes within many households in every year, and at any time, within the various household groupings, around a million children live in step-families (Utting, 1995: p. 22).

Children are increasingly likely to experience changing adult carers, and to find new formations of step-relatives added to their families, and existing relatives moving on to new relationships and households.

It is important to bear in mind that looking after children, a stressful time with many conflicting demands, may itself interlink with adverse circumstances. Households with children are more likely to be represented in low income groups, especially the households with only one adult, and there is a disproportionate number of households with children who are dependent on income support for their survival (Graham, 1994). Having children may well involve a financial struggle, and many children live at or below poverty levels. Family members may need to rely on each other to support and help in many different ways.

Overall, looking after children is a very substantial part of life for many people in the UK, and may involve considerable emotional, practical and financial struggles. The composition of households may differ between different ethnic groups; many households in the UK consist of only one adult, and there is an increasing possibility that the adults and children in the household will change over the period of childhood. Diversity and change are perhaps the hallmarks of the modern family, as there is a growing likelihood that the households of children, and the immediate carers of children, will change over the course of childhood. Accompanying these changes will be changes in grandparents, uncles, aunts and other members of *family*. The relevance of this network to family life will be considered after we review the situation of families who are involved with the social services.

## Families and social services

The Children Act 1989 laid a duty on local authorities to safeguard and promote the welfare of children who are *in need* and, as long as it was consistent with that child's welfare, to do so by supporting their family. A range of relevant services, not necessarily provided directly by the local authority, may be required to do this, and as we have already discussed, and as commentators suggested from the outset of the Act (Packman & Jordan, 1991), family support services have not had a very high priority over the past decades. Nonetheless it is an important step that the underlying philosophy of the Children Act is to identify and support those children who require more than the universal services, and that this support should be provided in the context of their family's care. It recognises the need for individually based services alongside universal provision, and the fact that those services should be an inclusive part of family life. It is estimated that around 600 000 out of the 10 million children in England are likely to fall in the 'in need' definition (Department of Health, 1995b).

Children whose welfare is at risk will fall into many categories. Child welfare issues are, for example, very likely to be involved with many of those young people who commit crimes and are caught up in the juvenile justice system; some 100 000 young people are cautioned each year, and a further 50 000 found guilty in the courts (Audit Commission, 1996: p. 11). Many of the children whose parents separate will also face quite substantial problems (Mitchell, 1985; Cocket & Tripp, 1994). Those who are the *victims* of crime are also at risk (Morgan & Zedner, 1992), and perhaps one in ten children will be such a victim each year (Central Statistical Office, 1994: p. 47). There are those in hospital with chronic illnesses, those excluded from school and so on. There will be many overlaps between these groups, but it is a substantial number of children who, each year, find their welfare at risk. The key fact is that the great majority of these young people will be living at home, and their family, while in part perhaps the cause of the problems, will be the main agency trying to resolve them. Any consequences of their problems will almost certainly be worked out in the context of their families. Families, broadly understood, are the major child welfare service.

### Using the social services

As we have discussed before it is a very small group of children who receive substantial services from social services departments. For example, out of the 10 million children in England, there were, in 1995, around 49 000 children looked after by local authorities (Department of Health, 1996), and around 35 000 on the child protection register, some of whom will also be looked after (Department of Health, 1995b). The stresses on the quite small numbers of *cared for* or *child protection* families are likely to be high (see Bebbington & Miles, 1989), but the great majority of these families are still very involved in their children's lives.

Families themselves take a good measure of responsibility in bringing the welfare of children to the attention of social services. For example in child protection work, Gibbons and her colleagues (Gibbons *et al.*, 1995) found that 17% of the 160 000 initial referrals to the child protection system were from 'family'. There were also 12% of referrals from people classified as 'other', and 6% were anonymous referrals. A number of these would presumably have been from extended family. This is the percentage at the entry point to the system.

As the cases progress through the assessments so more families are filtered out of the system altogether: of the 160 000 child protection referrals only around one in seven receive a service (Department of Health, 1995a). The family referral to child protection appears to become more and more prominent as the cases are filtered out by the system. Farmer and Owen (1995), in their study of child protection conferences, found that by the time the 160 000 had been reduced to around 40 000 conferences, the percentage of family member referrals was much higher than at the initial stage. Bearing in mind that their sample was small, it is a sharp contrast that over 50% of conferences in their study featured family referrals, as compared with around 20% of referrals at the outset of the child protection process. Perhaps family members feature strongly among the more reliable, serious and persistent referrers.

It is certainly the case that family members are 'the most important resources available' once children are inside the child welfare system (Bullock *et al.*, 1993: p. 67). They provide practical support and care, but also they are likely to be seen as having substantial influence over behaviour. The Audit Commission study of youth crime, for example, found that parents, brothers and sisters all rated highly in young offenders' eyes as influential, along with some acknowledgement of other family, including grandparents, aunts and uncles (Audit Commission, 1996: p. 63).

Of course some families will be struggling harder than others to look after the welfare of their children, and as we will discuss later, support is not directly predictable on the basis of kin relationships (Finch & Mason, 1993). Some family members will fail to support, and some will abuse and neglect their children. Children will be and should be removed from this minority, but except perhaps in a tiny minority of cases it is a *family member*, and not *family*, in the broad sense understood here, who has failed in this manner. For those children who enter the care system, the very tip of the iceberg of the problems, and the ones where home care has failed in significant ways, even for these children well over 80% are likely to be restored to their families for at least a short period (Bullock *et al.*, 1993: p. 67). From a policy and practice viewpoint it is clear that families need support not replacement.

## Help and the family

Voices can be heard, particularly in the media, suggesting that some of the changes in family structure or style have led to a collapse of family life and to the end of the support and the control that family members provided for each other in the past. This is not a new argument. A 'crisis' regarding the state of the family as a caring institution has been documented for many years. Moroney (1976), for example, cites the 'crisis' covered by the Royal Commission on the Poor Law in 1832, and there have been continual crises, ever since. Trying to assess the current state against the past is an almost impossible task, as social, spiritual, cultural and economic changes make comparisons relatively meaningless. However we have seen how central the family still is to children's lives, and the case for providing support, especially for parenting, is a strong one (see for example Utting *et al.*, 1993; Utting, 1995, 1996). But what would such a development build on as regards day-to-day support given by family members one to another? As we have already noted there is relatively little contemporary research on the social consequences of kinship, especially as regards child welfare. However the picture is starting to change. For example, recent research by McGlone and his colleagues (1996) has greatly illuminated this area and the discussion below is indebted to their work. The picture that emerges is one of a central role for the nuclear family, but also of a network of extended family that is of great importance, and where there can be a wide range of family members doing a great deal with each other and for each other.

### Who is where?

Living with your relatives, apart from your partner, spouse or dependant child, may not be very common, but the percentages doing so are still quite large. For example one third of those with adult children currently live with one or more of them. Equally it may be felt that people now move away from relatives for social, economic or other reasons, but in fact around 60% of people live within an hour's journey time from at least one close relative, and between a quarter and a third live less than 15 minutes away. Most commonly the family member in closest proximity is an adult child (McGlone *et al.*, 1996: pp. 55–56). Many of these people may of course be the aunts and uncles of the children with welfare problems.

Relatively close contact is maintained with non-resident relatives as shown in Table 2.1. Contact with adult children rivals that with 'best friend' and wide family contact is quite likely on a weekly basis.

There is no indication that things have changed dramatically in recent years. The figures are, for example, very similar to those found in 1986, although they are slightly lower in every category. It appears that

**Table 2.1** Frequency of seeing non-resident relatives/friends.

| | Daily (%) | At least once per week (%) | At least once per month (%) | Less often (%) | Never (%) | n |
|---|---|---|---|---|---|---|
| Mother | 8 | 40 | 21 | 27 | 3 | 1026 |
| Father | 6 | 33 | 20 | 29 | 9 | 822 |
| Adult sibling | 4 | 25 | 21 | 45 | 4 | 1702 |
| Adult child | 10 | 48 | 16 | 18 | 1 | 812 |
| Other relative | 3 | 31 | 26 | 37 | 1 | 1796 |
| Best friend | 10 | 48 | 22 | 17 | — | 1768 |

n = number of respondents
*From* McGlone *et al.*, 1996: p. 57.

there has been a small reduction in overall social contact, affecting both family and friends. But alongside this change has been the development of a different form of contact, the telephone. Nearly three in four parents speak to their son or daughter by telephone at least once per week (McGlone *et al.*, 1996: p. 57).

There is a considerable amount of family interaction and contact, much of it outside the immediate household. But what about helping? The great majority of this will obviously go on within the household, but as we discussed there are a range of outside services that could be relevant. In making a theoretical choice of who they would like to turn to, do people generally want to seek help outside their family?

## Who might help?

It appears to be far more likely that people will choose family, rather than friends or professionals, as a first source of help, even for depression or marital problems (Table 2.2). Friends do feature importantly, but the only professionals that receive any significant mention are the banks in connection with borrowing money, and even here over half would turn to their family.

Traditional roles still seem to apply, so for example, men are more likely than women to rely on a spouse/partner to help them while they are ill, and women more likely than men to rely on friends or children. Overall, there is a strong expressed commitment to family caring. The commitment seems to be more than just notional, more than just a feeling that this is 'what family should do'. When people were asked about the actual giving or receiving of help McGlone *et al.* (1966: p. 64) found that 19% had received care from a spouse/partner, 34% from parent/parent-in-law, and 22% had received care from another family

**Table 2.2**   Who would you turn to first for help regarding...?

| | Household job (%) | Help while ill (%) | Depression (%) | Marital problems (%) | Borrowing money (%) | n |
|---|---|---|---|---|---|---|
| Family | 83 | 88 | 68 | 53 | 51 | |
| Friend | 7 | 5 | 21 | 27 | 2 | |
| Bank | — | — | — | 45 | 32 | |
| Professionals | — | — | — | — | — | |
| | | | | | | 2077 |

n = number of respondents
From McGlone et al., 1996: p. 61.

member in the past year (10% from 'friends' and 5% from 'neighbours'). Equally the following had given care, 46% of spouses/partners, 16% of parents/parents-in-law, and 19% of 'other family members' (8% from 'friends' and 2% from 'neighbours').

But as with the earlier discussion about the current households of children, there is a good measure of diversity in the support given. There are indications that support for child care between family members may be stronger in working class families (F. McGlone, personal communication). It may be different for girls as compared with boys (Bost et al., 1994). There is some evidence that men's roles may vary according to perceived models of what families 'should be'. Dench, for example, has argued that there may be two broad patterns of family culture operating in modern Britain, that of the *traditional* family and that of the *alternative* family, with rather different consequences as to whether or not men accept more of the traditional tasks and responsibilities of women (Dench, 1996). In the traditional family obligations and rights are seen as deriving from some form of given rules, whereas the alternative family introduces an element of negotiation into these matters. Others have argued that there is an increasing impact of long work hours on family interaction, where, for example, fathers who worked more than 50 hours a week were markedly less likely to be involved in family activities (Ferri & Smith, 1996). It is clear that there is both variety and change.

Diversity is again the hallmark of the modern family, with values, employment patterns, culture, race and many other factors interacting and resulting in a unique blend for each family. The common feature is that family plays a prominent role in modern life, and a pivotal one in child welfare. It is clear that the family is a very important, and dominant, institution in modern Britain. There is wide variation, but the universal factor is that kinship is a very strong practical force in people's lives.

## The meaning of family

But what does *family* mean to its members? We have seen that, despite long-standing commentaries to the contrary, the concept of family as a group of inter-related people with varying degrees of obligations to each other has survived the many social changes taking us through to the late twentieth century. It is a dominant component of people's everyday discussions, and the interconnection between self and family is very important, as a recent study reported:

> 'In talking about events that matter, people are almost as likely to talk about something that has happened to other family members as they are to talk about themselves. People living alone or alone with children are as likely to mention other family members as those who live in "family households".'

> (Scott & Brook, 1997)

The family still has meaning, but the increasingly diverse forms and cultures of family make it difficult for policy makers and practitioners alike to know how to work with or for the family. Taking any one sociological definition will lead to insensitivity to different cultures and the exclusion of some families from consideration. Kinship is in part a social entity which is

> 'neither static nor uniform; its boundaries are permeable, depending on the circumstances in which individuals, couples, and elementary families find themselves. Its membership – and even this term implies too strong a boundary around it – is liable to change over time as people's interests and commitments, both inside and outside the family sphere alter. In particular, its make-up changes as people move through the life-course, adopting new roles and developing their relationships in new ways.'

> (Allan, 1996: p. 34)

For practitioners working with children and adolescents a flexible definition of family is needed, to encourage inclusive culture-sensitive alliances to work in the best interests of the child. Such a definition needs to work from the family's perspective, rather than being based on the assumptions or knowledge base of the professional. As Turner (1978: p. 137) argues:

> 'whether an individual is or is not part of the family becomes ... not a question of sociological definition of the family but rather a question of the extent of psychosocial influence a particular person exerts on the family.'

This approach then alerts us to the range of significant others who might be considered part of the intimate family, who may or may not be

kin. It is only the individuals within the family group itself who can
define the circle of people who have significance and who can therefore
be described as part of the family group. To work with the family, we
have to ask the family who the family is.

This view of the family as a psychosocial entity allows for change
over time as people take on different roles and new influences are
encompassed over the family life cycle. It allows us to see how *family*
survives and has meaning for its members, and it enables us to see that
the family group may vary from the point of view of different members
of the family. It also alerts us to the dangers of assuming that we know
about the family of our child welfare clients.

In order to understand the importance of working with the family,
we need to consider the impact of the wider family group on the
individual member. Firstly, what *meaning* does family have for the
child in their developing understanding of their self in the world, and
secondly what *impact* does this wider social world have on individual
members of the group. These two aspects of family will now be discussed in more detail: the family as a source of identity, and as a group
of individuals embedded in a social context.

## *Identity*

The individual state we call *identity* is based on a continuity of self
experience, a sense of who and what we are which is relatively stable
and allows each person to feel secure in being *me*. The concept of *me-
ness* or *self* develops throughout childhood and adolescence, starting
with the infant beginning to identify him- or herself as something
separate from others. Erikson (1963) described identity as the synthesis
of the individual experiences of passing through the developmental
stages, from infancy, through middle childhood and adolescence, to
adulthood. The *source* of experience is the child's interactions with the
outside world, their social and environmental contexts. Thus the self
concept is based on the evaluated beliefs a person holds about him- or
herself, and is thought to be of central importance to the individual
because all aspects of behaviour depend on the perception and organisation of past experiences. As Hassall (1994: p. 4) puts it: 'there is a
need for children to be guaranteed a place, a place in their family, a
place in their culture, a place in their local society, and a place in the
world'.

Identity is about the stability of self in the social world: 'to know
one's identity permits the comprehension of one's past, the potential-
ities of one's future and of one's place in the order of things' (Burns,
1979: p. 34). The individual's identity is dependent on, and derives
from, interactions with influential people and institutions. As Giddens
(1991: p. 53) has described it, there is a 'project of the self' consisting of
'the sustaining of coherent yet continuously revised biographical nar-

ratives'. Each person derives their identity from their interpretation of themselves in their context.

## The family as source of identity

The most influential experiences for the young individual will be those obtained within the psychosocial family group. It is within the family that the child gains a sense of permanence and continuity: the family provide the 'biographical narratives' that Giddens describes, the historical context of the individual. The importance of knowing about blood ties stems from the uniqueness of those ties to the self; nobody else has that history or place in the scheme of things. For most of us, perhaps, the historical context is a living fact, or given reality, and connections with past family figures and cultures are part of our identity without us appreciating it. But for those with disrupted family lives the absence of a personal history may leave a sense of 'not quite belonging'. For example for adopted children, as Haimes and Timms (1985: p. 2) comment, their 'curiosity about family history is readily understandable; it is by no means curious ... answering the question "Who am I?" seems to require some reference to background'. In their study, adoptees seeking information about their birth families were not seen as different or maladjusted but as trying to establish their place within social relations, to explain their difference as individuals unable to account fully for themselves. Children in care are to some extent similarly cut off from the continuity of experience that gives them their sense of self. People in these situations may feel different. It is more difficult for them to find their place in the order of things. They may have a precarious sense of self, due to incomplete or insecure narratives of themselves. They may also experience themselves as having a 'spoiled identity' (Goffman, 1963), feeling a distance between their experience of self and the 'normal'.

Ironically this very dissonance may be one of the reasons that social workers have tended to espouse the theory of the importance of family context rather more than doing the practical actions to make sure it is given due importance – theory and practice have not been closely linked. It was suggested around 20 years ago (Rautenam, 1976) that social workers sometimes shied away from helping people, especially children, to understand their past because of a desire to protect them from the knowledge of rejection or abandonment. Social workers are probably much better at discussing such difficult issues now, but they are still usually in a position to *interpret* things for their clients, and to *protect* them from the truth. As we have seen, taking on the partnership role in exploring difficulties in the real world with families and children is still more of a theoretical ideal rather than a reality. Yet the reality of the individual's life is the necessary history to provide a continuity of self – not being honest in working with people is to muddy the picture of that individual's or group's place in the order of things.

### The impact of wider social systems on identity

Although the family in its broad sense is recognised as a major influence on children, parents do not perhaps have the all-encompassing influence that was once thought. The study of child and adolescent development has moved over the years from considering the individual, through studying the importance of early attachment relationships to the consideration of wider social influences. Thus, the child's social supports and networks are now thought to be important in enlarging the social experiences that contribute to self identity: we discover that significant others are significant. The studies reported by Tavecchio and van IJzendoorn (1987) for example, show the positive effects of 'extended rearing contexts' and maternal employment with stable non-parental care on the security and resilience of young children. Extended kin are highlighted as important in many studies, such as those by Cochran and Riley (1990) and Furman and Buhrmester (1985). Siblings seem to be important sources of self perceptions for children as young as 3 (Kirchner & Vrondraek, 1975) extending the view already widely held of their importance in the development of identity in later childhood.

The extent of the influence of social networks, exerted in small friendship groups and through identification with specific groups of peers and participation in different activities, has recently been explored widely (see for example Nestmann & Hurrellmann, 1994; Crockett & Crouter, 1995; Cotterell, 1996). Aspects of these experiences will be incorporated into the individual's developing understanding of self. For example, group membership of adolescents at high school has been found to influence the continuing concept of self in relation to institutions and communities (Eckert, 1995). In a broader context still, the effect of the individual's culture and class environment on identity is discussed by Kim and associates (1994). Some writers have suggested that the development of identity is more complex in the 1990s than it has ever been. Giddens (1991), for example, argues that the pluralism and globalism of modern life ('modernity') offers choices about lifestyle which were previously unavailable to the individual, and which are increasingly important in the constitution of self identity.

Common to writings about identity is the recognition of the need for continuity, stability and coherence, alongside diversity, in the individual's interactions with the social world. All elements of social support are taken together by the child to suggest and sustain a sense of what is permanent and enduring (Boyce, 1985). For policy makers and practitioners, the key issue is helping children to find a way to recognise and utilise the social support networks that will maintain a sense of continuity and stability.

## *The family in context*

The child's perception of self is influenced by the family group of significant others, by peer relationships and community allegiances, but the family itself is not a closed system of relationships. It can be seen to be connected to, and affected by reciprocal interactions with, a very wide variety of other individuals and institutions. Bronfenbrenner (1979) described the child as being at the hub of a nested set of structures moving from the individual, micro system, through the meso- and exo-systems of family, school, church, work and leisure to the macro-systems of the political and financial worlds. This model of the child and family in an ecosystem of influences gives a view of the complexity and interdependence of the social structures available in the modern world. Paolucci *et al.* (1977: p. 22) suggested that 'the more complex an ecosystem the more successfully it can survive and resist stress', that is, the more the family is linked in to the social world at all levels, the more able it is to respond to difficult or unexpected circumstances. Conversely, it is suggested that the family without a complex social network may be more vulnerable and less able to find the resources to cope with crises. Bronfenbrenner's model also views the family as an entity influenced by the political and social environment, by employment levels, state benefits systems, the availability of alcohol and drugs, and so on. This suggests that child maltreatment should be conceptualised as a social-psychological phenomenon, shifting the emphasis away from a psychiatric or psycho-pathological model of child abuse, towards a recognition of the importance of the 'family in context' within child welfare work (Belsky, 1980).

### *The impact of social networks on the family*

There is considerable empirical evidence to support the ecological model of social systems and networks impacting on individuals and families. Social supports have been shown to have a positive impact on the aetiology and recovery from both physical and psychological illness, the so called *buffer effect* (see for example Cohen & Syme, 1985). The pioneering early work of Bott (1957) looked at the effects of family structure and kin ties on conjugal relationships, and included the warning that welfare workers and clinicians could add to a family's difficulties if, in trying to help, they did not take account of allegiances and responsibilities within the wider family network. This work led to studies showing increasingly complex interactions of influence between individuals, families and social support systems. Where early research often used the existence of a single intimate confiding relationship as the measure of social support, more recent studies have taken a much broader view of this support. Even apparently peripheral actors may, in connection with specific individuals and specific circumstances, play a

central role – for example, Cowen's (1982) work on the informal
supportive role taken by hairdressers and bartenders. More generally,
Cochran and colleagues' (1990) review of research on the social networks of parents and children separated out the different strands that
influence the building and maintenance of social networks in different
social groups. Cochran himself puts forward hypothesised relationships between network characteristics and developmental outcomes for
children. In his scheme, links with kin, non-kin, same age peers and
older peers, school and neighbourhood all have positive effects on
social and cognitive processes. Looking at wider community influences,
Parke and Kellam (1994) gather together research and theory on
relationships between family and social contexts, particularly work and
school, demonstrating the interconnectedness of different levels and
strands of the network. The social impact of the outside world will vary
widely and diversity is again the order of the day.

### Sources and functions of social networks

Support for parents is likely to come from a variety of different levels:
immediate family, friends and extended family and professional or
community support (Culbertson & Schellenbach, 1992). Any one
family might not recognise their sources of support until they face a
situation of need, and are forced by the demands of life stresses to call
upon those resources available. Cochran *et al.* (1990) discuss this as the
concept of 'press'. However, different families will have access to different networks and have varied attitudes to calling upon them for help.
The preferred source of support will depend upon many different factors such as those discussed by Orford (1992) concerning the importance of availability, adequacy, stability, reliability and timing. Studies
of family networks and support have shown the complex set of attitudes and expectations, through which the wider family interactions
are negotiated (Finch & Mason, 1993).

Just as the possible sources of support are varied, so are the functions
of social support varied. And similarly, different functions may be more
or less important to individuals at different times. There has been
considerable debate about the categories of social support functions,
much of which appears to be due to semantic differences. The range of
functions are generally agreed to be:

- Material, tangible or instrumental support or aid
- Emotional, expressive or affect support, or caring
- Esteem, affirmation or value support, or acknowledgement
- Informational, advice, or cognitive support, or guidance
- Companionship support, or positive social interaction (Orford,
  1992: p. 65)

Cohen and colleagues (1985) developed a measure of the functional components of social support, and investigated the relative value of the functions as potential social resources. They found that material support may be less influential as a buffer to life events than esteem and informational support, but they argue that

> 'the effectiveness of any particular support resource may well depend on the context of the situation... The match between the needs elicited by the stressful events one encounters and available support is central to understanding when a particular kind of support will be a successful buffer.'

> (Cohen *et al.*, 1985: p. 89)

The terms social support and social network can therefore be seen to encompass a wealth of relationships in the lives of families with kin, peers, work mates, teachers, family friends, community workers, local characters and other professionals. The preferred sources and functions of social support in situations of stress therefore depend upon many factors including the stage of the family life cycle, the negotiation and maintenance of network links and the particular history of the need for support. This makes it very difficult for anyone, professional or otherwise, to develop network support and help for a family in a prescriptive way. It is hard to anticipate which sources of support will be most appropriate, and which functions will be most beneficial. Policy makers and practitioners in social welfare need to help families identify and utilise their social supports and networks in the way that is most appropriate and beneficial for them and their children in their particular circumstances and contexts.

## Conclusions

It appears that we can again report, as Moroney did around 20 years ago, that 'the family appears to be stronger and more viable than many anticipated' (Moroney, 1976: p. 138). There is clearly a good deal of family support for social services, although maybe somewhat less the other way. As Utting's 'guide to the debate' about families has noted, 'although not so conspicuously close-knit as 30 years ago, extended families remain, with the aid of telephones and motor cars, a potent and insufficiently recognised source of social support' (Utting, 1995: p. 29). Both the nuclear family and the extended family are actively involved in the lives of children, providing care and support, and nearly always picking up the pieces when a family member neglects or abuses the children in their care. The practical side of the family is matched by the psychological one. The family group, in complex interaction with external factors and supports, gives meaning and identity, or as Hassall (1994) puts it 'a sense of place'.

For a practitioner or policymaker this discussion is likely to engender feelings that a greater focus on the wider importance and sense of the family is now needed – alongside a serious concern that providing this for each family in an appropriately comprehensive and unique way is a tall order. It also must be done within a frame that provides for proper professional assessment, so that a *bottom line* is made clear as regards children's welfare, within the legal powers and duties of the services. The Family Group Conference was developed as one practical way to address these issues, and the origins and key dimensions of the Conferences form the subject of the next chapter.

# Chapter 3

# Family Group Conferences: Policy and Practice

This chapter covers the background and origin of Family Group Conferences, and discusses the way that the UK programme developed their use in child welfare. It provides an outline of the main dimensions of the Conferences, the pillars on which they rest. It discusses the process of the Conferences, highlighting the differences that there are with other forms of meetings. The last sections of the chapter provide a rough guide to co-ordinating Family Group Conferences, adding another piece to the picture of Conferences that we began to draw with the outline in Chapter 1.

## The background of Family Group Conferences

The origins of Family Group Conferences lie in New Zealand in the early 1980s, although the pressures and ideas that led to them have been occurring throughout the Western world (Hassall & Maxwell, 1991). Many of these ideas also underpin the Children Act 1989, whose underlying philosophy supports Family Group Conferences very well (Marsh, 1994, 1996; Marsh & Crow, 1996).

The broad themes that lay behind Family Group Conferences represent changes in societal views about children and families, and a growing recognition of professional difficulties, and often short-comings, in protecting children's welfare. There are positive elements regarding the role of children and families, and more negative ones regarding the relative failure of existing services and the approach underlying them.

The first theme involves the increasing concern about child abuse, a topic which has become much more prominent in public and policy debates. This prominence has been accompanied by a growing realisation that the professional policies and practices designed to protect children can themselves be harmful.

The second theme has been the importance of encouraging parental accountability and responsibility: the idea that policies and services have perhaps taken over functions and roles which were previously carried out by the family. Alongside this, problems of public care of children have become all too apparent, for example the tragic stories of abuse of children in residential care; when children are cared for away from their parents it does not always seem to improve matters. With increasing regularity the adult care of children has been seen as neglectful of its responsibilities, but professional answers seem to have their pitfalls as well.

A third theme has been concerned with the need to increase young people's involvement and accountability in ways that are meaningful to them and to society. Discussion of children's rights, for example around their control of medical examination of their bodies, has been increasingly evident. Child welfare services on the other hand, despite some legal changes in this direction, seem to have lagged behind in their involvement of children, and to have struggled to find ways to give young people a voice in services so that their views are not solely expressed by either professionals or parents.

Finally there have been issues regarding youth crime, and the trend towards focusing work with offenders quite explicitly on the offending, with accountability well to the fore again. Services have been seen as falling uncomfortably between the stools of welfare and justice, and as failing to make young offenders, and perhaps their parents, account-able. Increasingly it has also been evident that justice processes are not dealing very well with victims of crime, and the need to move towards a more restorative form of justice (Burnside & Baker, 1994; Walgrave, 1995) and to provide something in the way of reparation has become more prominent as an issue.

As these themes have been worked out in policy and practice debates a number of responses have developed, for example the growth of mediation within justice services, the increase in children's involvement in planning meetings, the development of appeals regarding profes-sional child protection services or the growth of home-based volunteer programmes like Home Start in the UK. But in one country in particular – New Zealand – the debates had a particular focus, which led to the development and implementation of the Family Group Conference model.

## The development in New Zealand

The pressures and ideas recounted above were as prominent in New Zealand as in the UK, with perhaps a particular emphasis on increasing involvement and participation, but the debates that encompassed them had a sharper focus on the family, and in particular on the extended family. This was primarily due to the consistent objections from Maori that the needs of their children were being very badly dealt with by the child welfare system, and that it would be far better to support Maori families rather than to remove their children, a process which all too often reduced or severed the children's links with their families.

Maori culture emphasises the extended family's key role in bringing up children. There was an outcry that something should be done to help strengthen, rather than weaken, children's crucial kinship links: the *whanau*, *hapu* and *iwi*, which are the Maori kinship groupings, and which can be translated very loosely as extended families, clans and tribes (Connolly, 1994; Hassall, 1996). This strongly expressed view was accompanied by the growing realisation, shared worldwide, that the quality of care and protection provided by the state was often not very good and was sometimes worse than that provided by the family that the child had left (see for example the report on sexual abuse within the New Zealand child care system, in von Dadelszen, 1987).

There was a prominent and public championing of the need to strengthen families and to respect family culture, which was perhaps unique. But this stance needed some means of enactment, and accompanying the growing concerns there was experimentation in a number of social services offices with the involvement of families directly in the work of the multidisciplinary child protection teams (Hassall, 1996: pp. 21–22). This provided a context of both problem and solution, but the fact that it resulted in major change was both the result of cumulative improvements in reform proposals and, at least in part, serendipitous events.

A series of reviews of the child welfare legislation had produced ideas for sound but relatively unadventurous reforms. Nonetheless within the ideas there was, or there was at least claimed to be, an increasing role for family decision-making within the welfare system. However there was continuing criticism that the proposals failed to address the major problems. There was vociferous condemnation on the grounds that it failed to respond to the need for Maori to be given back control over their own children, and the practitioner experiments continued to develop increased family decision-making within the welfare system. Towards the end of a 5-year process a combination of the report of a creative working party, pressure for change and a committed Minister achieved legislation whose radical nature was probably not fully appreciated at the time. The Children, Young Persons and their Families Act 1989 had at its heart a model of decision-making called a Family Group Conference. It was a mandatory requirement for serious child welfare cases, and for all youth justice cases whenever criminal proceedings are contemplated or brought (for some of the underlying youth justice issues see Maxwell & Morris, 1993: pp. 1–7). In response to the concerns about the victims of crime, and their lack of involvement in justice processes, the youth justice Conferences included victims as key partners, an area we shall discuss in more detail later.

A new and radical innovation was introduced throughout the child welfare and youth justice services in New Zealand; it was, as one leading commentator put it, 'a bold break with the past' (Atkin, 1991: p. 392). Although it built on some existing practice it nonetheless represented a major move towards empowering families, and in youth justice towards involving victims. New jobs of co-ordinators were to be created throughout the country, and many new structures erected to carry out the comprehensive changes envisaged by the Act.

All of this was done in a very short time scale, and the Act continued its development in the context of New Zealand's permanent revolution in government, where experimental market models have been introduced into nearly all areas of public service, including child welfare, with mixed results (Kelsey, 1995). The nation-wide Children and Young Persons' Service was subjected to annual re-organisations, and it struggled to make sure that the Act was properly implemented. There was little training available, social workers' qualifying training did not alter very fast, co-ordinators found themselves in new jobs with little support, and yet despite substantial rough edges the Act, and the model of practice at its heart, has received continuing endorsement, for example from a major governmental review (Mason *et al.*, 1992).

There was, and there continues to be, an almost unique opportunity in New Zealand for research into this substantial natural experiment. Sadly, on the child welfare side, this has not really been taken up. Figures for child placement for some years before and after the Act, for example, prove generally skimpy or somewhat unreliable. The child welfare research that has been carried out has been limited in focus (see Chapter 5), and at the time of writing the only comprehensive proposal for a major outcome study, developed partly with government, still remains unfunded (Maxwell *et al.*, 1995).

## *The development in Oregon*

In 1989, at around the same period that the New Zealanders were beginning to implement their new legislation and its Family Group Conferences, the Children's Services Department in Portland, Oregon, was beginning to try out a model of practice with some similarities, the Family Unity Meeting (Graber *et al.*, 1996). This approach was based on a firm commitment to seek and support the strengths of families who are experiencing child welfare problems. Many factors distinguish these meetings from other child care planning meetings, perhaps principally a strong desire to listen to family solutions, and wherever appropriate to support them.

In the Family Unity Meetings *problems* are rethought as *issues of concern*; they are considered alongside an assessment of family strengths and options that the family has thought about, with relevant ideas (not advice) from professionals, or jointly developed in the meetings if that is appropriate. At the end of a meeting a *touch points partnership* work sheet outlines in visual form who will do what to take the ideas forward.

There is therefore some shared philosophy between these meetings and Family Group Conferences, but also some substantial differences, principally that the family does not have time on their own, that extended family is not emphasised as strongly, and that the co-ordination of the meeting is carried out by service staff. As time has gone on the links between the Family Unity Meeting and the Family Group Conference have grown and more of the Conference approach has been incorporated.

One of the key lessons from the Oregon programme is around implementation. From the earliest stages it was emphasised that values underpinning the model needed to be discussed widely, and that it was preferable if the whole agency reflected the policies of respect, and seeking out of strengths, that were part of the model (Graber *et al.*, 1996). These issues have been reflected in reports on the use of values material in partnership training in the UK (Newton & Marsh, 1993) and in the need for staff at all levels to be involved if partnership type developments are to be properly enacted (Stevenson & Parsloe, 1993).

## The focus of the UK programme

The UK programme was based on the experience in New Zealand, drawing on ideas from Oregon and from other partnership develop-ments, but developed in the context, and firmly located in the philo-sophy, of the Children Act 1989 (Marsh, 1994, 1996; Marsh & Crow, 1996). It drew on the major developments of the Act, such as the need for careful consideration of children's voices, the increased emphasis on 'race, religion, language and culture', the focus on links between chil-dren and their families, and the overall emphasis on the partnership between families and services. The involvement of the Family Rights Group was central to the work, as was the interest of the practitioners and managers in social services who were prepared to put the time and effort into the substantial changes involved. All of these factors con-tributed to the development being primarily around social services' work in child welfare, and there was not an equivalent programme in youth justice, despite its prominent place in New Zealand.

### Youth justice

Family Group Conferences play a central role in youth justice in New Zealand (Stewart, 1996), but although plans have been outlined for their development in England and Wales (Allen, 1996) they have been slow to take off. There are reasons to think that they would be relevant to some of the problems that currently face the youth justice system (Audit Commission, 1996: p. 50) and that they may play a role in strengthening families that would have some impact on encouraging young offenders to stop offending (Graham & Bowling, 1995: p. 102). Perhaps two key features stand out: the possibility of establishing much more clearly the accountability of offenders, and the opportunity to increase the involvement of victims, and potentially increase their satisfaction with both process and outcome of the youth justice system.

It must be borne in mind that the youth justice Conferences have two distinctive additional dimensions alongside those in child welfare. First, they are inextricably intertwined with a youth justice legislative base and a criminal justice system that does not share much of their philosophy. The major impact of this factor may be around issues of implementation. Secondly, and crucially, they are only indirectly concerned with the welfare of children, their primary focus is on the restoration of the torn social fabric that has occurred with the committing of a crime.

When property is stolen, or violence is committed, individual or group victims are directly affected. Even crimes that involve organisations have ramifications for the people involved, for example the store manager who is reprimanded for loose security, the store workers who have to clear up all the broken windows, or the psychological effects on staff of perceived or threatened violence. Restoring the situation to how it was before is impossible, but attempts to find ways to *make good* have throughout history been at the heart of much of the human, non-institutional, exchanges that occur when one person wrongs another. They have involved an exchange of words, or deeds, or money in the form of apologies, offers to clear up, making amends, replacing goods, and so on. The idea of a form of *restorative justice* to form a third variant of youth justice, different from retribution or rehabilitation, has gained ground in recent years (Walgrave, 1995) and it is central to the use of Family Group Conferences in the youth justice area. In a real and personal manner the offender, and their family, is engaged in trying to *make amends* with the victim, and possibly their family. In doing so they are of course accepting responsibility. Increasing offender accountability and improving the way that victims are dealt with in the system are both addressed by the restorative justice approach in the Family Group Conference.

The skills and approaches to do this are perhaps less akin to negotiation, which is so important to the welfare model, and more akin to mediation (Maxwell & Morris, 1993; pp. 4–7). Mediation will also have a role in the welfare work, but it is much more prominent in the youth justice model.

The Conference progresses along very similar lines to the welfare one, but with the additional components already mentioned. It will only take place if the offender has agreed that they are guilty, otherwise the case must first be argued in a court. In the New Zealand model it can take place either informally (*intention to charge*, which may not then be taken up if the Conference outcome is satisfactory), or formally (following a brief court appearance, or a substantial one to hear a not guilty plea) and then an adjournment to hear the outcome of a Conference. In common with the welfare Family Group Conference there must be unanimity of view at the end, but in this case the police, the offender and the victim all must feel that justice has been done.

Victims of course must be treated with great respect and care during the entire proceedings, as the opportunity for revictimisation exists. The early New Zealand experience was salutary in this respect and victims were often not properly notified or dealt with, they only attended half of the Conferences, and around one third were not particularly satisfied with the outcomes (Maxwell & Morris, 1993: pp. 118–122). The Conferences needed substantial improvements in this regard with much better notification, support and engagement of victims. There has been action on these areas in New Zealand, and other research indicates a very positive reaction from victims to the Conferences process (T. Goodes, personal communication).

Indeed putting the victim at the heart of the Conference is crucial to all aspects of its organisation. For example, it should be held at a place and time acceptable to the victim, the victim should be as fully prepared as any other member, supporters for the victim, especially their family, should be considered, and the full agreement of the victim to the outcome must be stressed. Victims and their family/supporters may, in common with offenders and their families, also want some private time on their own during the Conference. This can occur at the same point as the offender family having their private time on their own. Some victims want the co-ordinator to be present during this period as it can be used for victims to outline issues that they did not want to raise in the first part of the Conference, but which they would like considered in the last part, when agreement is being reached about what is to be done. Personal matters that they feel are not the province of the main meeting could, for example, be considered in this way. There is therefore a stage of victim time, which may at times be private consideration within the victim family/supporter group, to be added to the period when private family time occurs, and this is outlined in Fig. 3.1. The Rough Guide to co-ordinating Family Group Conferences later in this chapter covers these issues and the way that the victim could be involved without attending, for example by written statements. The overall process of the youth justice Family Group Conference is summarised in Fig. 3.1.

### Other areas

There are other areas that Family Group Conferences may well help, including adult care, adult justice and in particular the proceedings surrounding divorcing or separating couples. This idea has been proposed in New Zealand (Hassall & Maxwell, 1992, 1993) and this generated a lively critical debate (Abrams, 1992; Henaghan, 1992; Wellington District Family Law Committee, 1992). In fact the use of Family Group Conferences would seem to have something in common

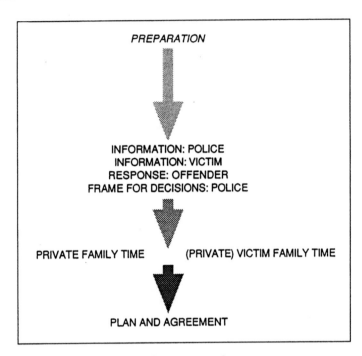

PREPARATION

INFORMATION: POLICE
INFORMATION: VICTIM
RESPONSE: OFFENDER
FRAME FOR DECISIONS: POLICE

PRIVATE FAMILY TIME        (PRIVATE) VICTIM FAMILY TIME

PLAN AND AGREEMENT

**Fig. 3.1**   The youth justice Family Group Conference.

with the Family Law Reform Act 1996, around the idea of children having an enduring link with family members, the preference for negotiated settlements and meetings of all parties. However the Family Law Reform Act 1996 has had to incorporate a series of hostile amendments, and it has been implemented with little consideration of the practical means for carrying it out; it looks as though it will not have much chance of success (Cretney & Masson, 1997: pp. 326–383). The contribution of Family Group Conferences to this area may be one of the ways that the Act could be improved over the years to come.

## Key dimensions of a Family Group Conference

We have considered the background to the Conferences, and some of the developments of them, and provided earlier, in Chapter 1, a brief outline of the Conference itself. In later sections of this chapter we provide a Rough Guide to co-ordinating Family Group Conferences, but before we turn to this it would be useful to cover the key dimensions of the Conference, the pillars on which it rests.

The dimensions of the Conference listed below address the main points that lay behind their development and which we covered in Chapters 1 and 2: the idea of gathering better information for considerations of seriousness, increasing levels of family involvement in decision-making, improving the commitment to the decisions that are ference. In common with the welfare Family Group Conference there must be unanimity of view at the end, but in this case the police, the offender and the victim all must feel that justice has been done.

Victims of course must be treated with great respect and care during the entire proceedings, as the opportunity for revictimisation exists. The early New Zealand experience was salutary in this respect and victims were often not properly notified or dealt with, they only attended half of the Conferences, and around one third were not particularly satisfied with the outcomes (Maxwell & Morris, 1993: pp. 118–122). The Conferences needed substantial improvements in this regard with much better notification, support and engagement of victims. There has been action on these areas in New Zealand, and other research indicates a very positive reaction from victims to the Conferences process (T. Goodes, personal communication).

Indeed putting the victim at the heart of the Conference is crucial to all aspects of its organisation. For example, it should be held at a place and time acceptable to the victim, the victim should be as fully prepared as any other member, supporters for the victim, especially their family, should be considered, and the full agreement of the victim to the outcome must be stressed. Victims and their family/supporters may, in common with offenders and their families, also want some private time on their own during the Conference. This can occur at the same point as the offender family having their private time on their own. Some victims want the co-ordinator to be present during this period as it can be used for victims to outline issues that they did not want to raise in the first part of the Conference, but which they would like considered in the last part, when agreement is being reached about what is to be done. Personal matters that they feel are not the province of the main meeting could, for example, be considered in this way. There is therefore a stage of victim time, which may at times be private consideration within the victim family/supporter group, to be added to the period when private family time occurs, and this is outlined in Fig. 3.1. The Rough Guide to co-ordinating Family Group Conferences later in this chapter covers these issues and the way that the victim could be involved without attending, for example by written statements. The overall process of the youth justice Family Group Conference is summarised in Fig. 3.1.

*Other areas*

There are other areas that Family Group Conferences may well help, including adult care, adult justice and in particular the proceedings surrounding divorcing or separating couples. This idea has been proposed in New Zealand (Hassall & Maxwell, 1992, 1993) and this generated a lively critical debate (Abrams, 1992; Henaghan, 1992; Wellington District Family Law Committee, 1992). In fact the use of Family Group Conferences would seem to have something in common

In this sense co-ordinators need to be independent. They might, of course, have comments to make about assessment or services, but they are not assessors and they are not providers. They should not see case files before Conferences, that is not their task; they should listen to family members, especially to children and young people. They must also make judgements as to whether some support may be needed for participants, for instance a family member acceptable to the young person who will be committed to speaking on that young person's behalf at a key point. Listening and support in this manner cannot be combined with the assessment work.

It may be best if they are paid and managed through an agency which is not the main assessing organisation, perhaps a voluntary body contracted to a social services department. This is more likely to give them a greater chance of being viewed as independent by family. The family needs to feel that they are, relatively, independent: that is the key issue. Family members need to see the co-ordinator as being in charge of the process, and not the input or the outcome of the Conference.

## Respect and support for family views, unless there is a risk of significant harm to the child

The need to achieve maximum levels of agreement needs to be put in the context of the professional duty under the Children Act 1989 to make sure that there is not a risk of significant harm to the child. For many Family Group Conferences this will not be a major issue, as they will not focus on acute concerns regarding the protection of children, but some of those that are the most worrying to professionals and family members will focus on such concerns. Professionals, and family members, will both be making judgements about the risks; it is a collaborative effort. Professionals must finally decide if there is a risk of significant harm in the light of the plans proposed. If they feel there is, and the plans cannot be altered to remove this, then their views will need to be tested in courts (with children in such circumstances very likely to have been placed in guaranteed safety before the Conference is held).

The overall stance is a respect for family views as key ingredients of the child welfare service. In general family members are child welfare workers alongside the professionals.

## Building on family strengths, and negotiation of services

The Conferences are oriented towards family strengths, and services need to support these strengths. In situations where there is inevitable consideration of child welfare problems this is not easy. Listing problems is, for nearly everyone, much easier than listing strengths. Sometimes strengths emerge, and we are surprised by them. Focusing on strengths is not an easy task.

Negotiating services may not be straightforward either. Almost everyone who is responsible for a service is likely to feel that it would be much more simple if people would accept what is there, as of course they often will. Negotiation can easily be seen as inefficient, as a delay which is really a waste of professional time. However, encouraging the negotiation of that service may actually pay dividends in getting the service used to its best advantage, and in not wasting time and resources on what is not really wanted.

## Youth justice: the central role of the victim

The dimensions outlined above are as relevant in youth justice as in child welfare, however there is the additional involvement of the victim, and this is central. It means that Conference process, place, timing and negotiation of outcome must all adapt. The process needs to be fully respectful to the victim, including consideration of the key issue of the need for the victim to be empowered and not disempowered by the Conference. The place, time and process of the Conference will revolve around the victim as well, in the context of the needs of the offender and their family. Balancing all of these demands is a difficult, but in practice not impossible, task.

## Diversity but conformity

Conferences should be different one from another because families are different, but they should be the same because their underlying principles are the same. They are the same in intent, and in broad outline format, but they are going to be very different in their feel, their content, their style. This is partly true of a traditional office meeting, where different personal interactions or agenda items will affect the meeting style, but in that type of meeting it happens mostly by default, not as a deliberate feature. Family Group Conferences should be diverse, within their principled base. The next section examines this diversity, and difference from other meetings, in more detail.

## The process of Family Group Conferences

Both the model of the Conference, and the dimensions covered above can seem to be related to other approaches to child welfare practice. They *are* related: it is an extension of partnership, it would benefit from mediation skills, it does do everything possible to be respectful to different cultures. Certainly the individual elements of the Family Group Conference model and its dimensions would be found in some of the best practice in child welfare. And yet there is something very different when all of the elements are present, and when there is a real Family

Group Conference. It is probably unnecessary to argue too long about differences and similarities, except to make sure that the claim is not made that one element alone makes a Family Group Conference. It does not. Family Group Conferences involve all of the elements specified, and an approach by the co-ordinator which we cover shortly in the Rough Guide. When this happens they do feel very different to the participants from existing, best, practice (we will cover more about the experience of them in later chapters). Expressing the difference in words is quite hard.

Consider this example. At one of the Family Group Conferences in the programme the young man who was the subject of the Conference said that he wanted to greet the Conference members as they came up the stairs (it was being held in an upstairs room in a sports centre). He did so by saying to each person 'welcome to my conference'. This was his way of doing things, it fitted the place, the family, the situation: it fitted that unique Conference.

## *Process, direction and uniformity*

Another way to approach the difference might be via analogy. There are, for example, a number of palpable differences between experiencing a play in a theatre and experiencing a film in a cinema. One of them is that the audience in the play engage with the actors, they know that things can go wrong, there is an element of risk. Each night will be different in some way from each other. Monday's audience appreciates the comic elements, and Tuesday's the tragic ones. On Wednesday the actors stumble with the words and the audience hold their breath as to what will happen....

No analogy can or should be carried too far, but the comparison with the theatre may be useful to convey the sense of occasion, the sense of frailty, the extraordinary mix of the comic and the tragic, the rapid move from the trivial to the vital, the changes in control, all of which mark out the Family Group Conference as quite distinctive. The director of a play can only do so much before the cast, from the leading actors to the bit players, must be trusted on their own. The director must work closely with set and lighting designers as part of a team. Stage-fright can paralyse an actor, and they will need a great deal of positive support. Different theatres have a quite different ambience and will make the same play seem different. Actors may forget lines and have to ad lib, and then slowly, in conjunction one with the other, work their way back to the script.

All of the following elements may be analogous to different aspects of the Conference; they are worth considering as a frame through which the differences from other forms of meeting can be examined:

- Director
- Leading actors

- Bit players
- Set and lighting designer
- Stage-fright problems
- Effect of different theatres on the same play
- The impact of ad libs
- The consequence of losing the plot

Conferences are performances where the sense of risk is palpable; where the setting and interaction are central. Like the best theatre they require great skills from all who take part, and in particular from the co-ordinator.

## Skill and difficulty

Co-ordinators may in practice be more like trainers than theatre directors. They must consider the aims and purposes of the event, convince people to come, make sure that participants are relatively at their ease, have materials on hand for recording key points, make sure the setting feels right, encourage participation, ensure that everything is understood and round off the event in a suitable manner. Co-ordinators need the skills of the very best trainers. What they need to do with these skills is covered next in a Rough Guide that was designed for the UK programme.

## A Rough Guide to co-ordinating Family Group Conferences

A guide for good practice in Family Group Conferences was developed as the programme progressed. It used the experience of families, social workers and co-ordinators as well as relevant research. It was constructed as a series of key points and practice hints, and not as a detailed manual (for an example of a manual see Pennell & Burford, 1995a, which focuses on the use of the Conferences in situations of domestic violence). The main headings in the guide often provided the focus for sections of the training programme. So, for example, training moved from a consideration of 'who is in the family?' to working out the best means to get them to actually attend the Conference. The detail of that programme is discussed in the next chapter.

Throughout the guide the best practice within child welfare work was assumed and where necessary re-emphasised: that proper respect is paid to the child's views at all times, that race, religion, language and culture are suitably covered and respected, and that all the proceedings are handled with decency, professionalism and care.

It would be useful to begin with a reminder about the key Conference stages, using the diagram we considered earlier (Fig. 3.2), before moving on to the sections of the guide.

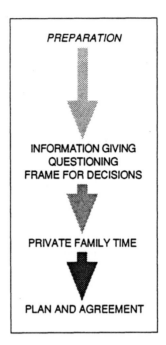

**Fig. 3.2** The Family Group Conference.

The UK programme's work focused exclusively on child welfare conferences, but in the version of the Guide given below some additional mention is also made of the needs of youth justice. With that exception everything which follows was the basis for training the co-ordinators in the project and the way it is reproduced here reflects that training base. It could be considered as a set of guidelines covering best practice in Family Group Conferences.

## Who is in the family?

The starting point for the work is to decide who is in the family, and the starting point for this is the child or young person's view. It is important to distinguish the question 'who is in the family?' from the quite different question 'who do you want to come to the Conference?', as the co-ordinator may need to do some very delicate negotiation about the latter. They can only do so if they are well informed about family membership beforehand. Information from other key informants, who must include adults with parental responsibility and carers of the child, will start to fill out the family picture. Soon it will become evident whether or not there is a core membership of the family, and whether or not there is significant conflict about membership, or between members.

The case notes for the family concerned are the business of the assessors, usually the social worker, and not of the co-ordinators. Apart from basic family details, names and addresses and telephones, the family will explain itself, principally through the eyes of the child or young person. Siblings may help young children to express a view, and for all family members a range of techniques to help them establish who is in the family will be useful. Discussion of major family events, such as weddings or separations, and who was involved and why, is likely to be helpful, and photographs may be available that will aid this process. Considering favourite things, and favourite places, may bring up family names, as may asking about birth place, or different homes that have been lived in. Encouraging as wide a view of family as possible is important in order that there can be proper discussion about who should come (and this in turn may influence the place and time of the Conference).

In the course of the discussions it should become clear if anyone is likely to need additional support. Does the child or young person need this? They might be encouraged to rehearse contributions, or to seek a family member they trust to support them. The co-ordinator needs to be very sensitive to the needs of those who are less powerful and how their voices will be heard, and to encourage and support full participation as appropriate.

## Getting them there

It is important to start with an approach that encourages attendance, as a positive attitude will to some degree be suitably infectious. Once begun, the process of inviting is not the sole responsibility of the co-ordinator, it is the family's conference, and many families will start to issue their own invitations themselves. Young people may want to do this for themselves. However family members may also try to exclude people, by not inviting them, and of course by simply not mentioning them. The co-ordinator has to bear in mind at all times the child's needs for access to their family, that they have an uncle, for example, even if the parent of the child wants to deny that fact.

Some family members will have more prominent roles in the process of inviting and respecting this may be important. They may also be prominent in excluding people, and understanding and dealing with this will also be important.

It may be useful for co-ordinators to develop a personal check list to ensure that the following points are covered in any correspondence or communication:

- Who you are (that you are not responsible for assessment or investigation)
- Why you are contacting them (desire to involve family in important decisions, concern for child)

- What any involvement will mean (the three stages of the Conference)
- What you are wanting (attendance, and not any expectation that they will care for the child)

All communications should be in the preferred language of the family member concerned.

The preparation for the Conference is a crucial stage. It sets the tone of the forthcoming meeting, it should ensure that good information is available, and it will enable the co-ordinator to stress and to restress the importance of focusing the meeting on the welfare of the child or young person.

## Keeping them out

The co-ordinator has the right, and responsibility, to exclude any family member from the Conference. They must also consider carefully the professional attendance, as only those with information to give about the child concerned, or those whose services are very likely to need explaining, should attend. Exclusion of family members should be on the basis of limited clear rules, for example that there is a proven likelihood of violence, that the person is drunk or under the influence of drugs at the time of the meeting, or that there is sound evidence of an inability to contribute because of mental health problems.

The child's view must be central to decisions about who to exclude, but, if possible, any concerns they express should be handled by providing support rather than excluding others. For example a family member the child likes and trusts could be approached to support that young person and to make sure that fears of intimidation are overcome. Ultimately it is the decision of the co-ordinator alone as to who should be excluded and who should be allowed to attend.

The intimidation of family members is an important issue, and the need for a supporter, preferably within the family, should always be considered if the co-ordinator thinks there is a risk of this.

It is possible that contributions can be made on paper, or via others, thus allowing the views of someone that should be excluded, or has excluded themselves, still to be heard.

## Priority of efforts

It is important to get the Conference under way reasonably quickly, as delay will usually be against the interests of the child or young person. Clearly there is a balance between who you can get to come to the Conference and the speed with which the Conference can be arranged. Some relatives, for example, may be hard to contact, or find it difficult to attend Conferences that are due to be held quickly. The judgement must focus on the need for speed against the need for key members to be present, and it will vary from circumstance to circumstance, although substantial delay will almost never be appropriate. The child's priorities for those attending may be very important in focusing the co-ordinator's efforts.

Professional attendance also needs careful consideration. It is vital to have those professionals present who have key information about the child, and to have those people whose services are very likely to be central to the child in the future. There is a possibility that the latter group may be contacted by telephone during the conference if attendance is very difficult.

### The art of the possible

There are many judgements to be made by co-ordinators, and they all need to be taken on the basis of the fundamental principles underlying Family Group Conferences, but they also need to be made on a realistic basis of getting the Conference under way and functioning. Knowing when to compromise and when not to is vital. Careful, and professionally sound, pragmatism may often be very important. Perhaps co-ordinators need to be reassured that Family Group Conferences are 'the art of the possible'.

## Engaging the family

There is a great deal of personal style involved in this process (see Chapter 7). The co-ordinator needs to be firm but respectful, and although there are very serious issues involved they will need to introduce a little lightness into the process at times – encouraging participation means recognising that both humour and gravity may have their part to play.

There is a risk of becoming overinvolved in the family's own decision-making process, and remembering that the co-ordinator *co-ordinates* and does not orchestrate is crucial.

Ideally, there should be no surprises for the co-ordinator or the family in the information presented at the start of the meeting, as everything should have been discussed, at least in outline, beforehand. Clearly this is a counsel of perfection, but it is a standard to be strived for. Brief premeetings may help with this, as long as they do not in any way usurp the Conference itself. These meetings may also be used to resolve adult conflicts that are clearly going to occur, although the evidence is that these are much more likely to impinge on attendance rather than on the meeting itself (see Chapter 6).

Engagement will involve gathering some sense of alliances and conflicts, and in the context of these being able to put clearly the basic ground rules about the Conference. It is vital to be crystal clear that the

Conference is about the child's welfare, as compared with, for example, past family battles or complaints about social services. These other issues may affect the welfare of the child, and they will need to be considered, but they are not the purpose of the Conference.

Engagement also involves sensitivity to the range of ways that people interact, and some of the symbolism of that interaction, for example the use of food. The word companionship comes from the sharing of bread, and the use of food, even of cups of tea, may be crucial to engaging the family. Providing food allows for a different sort of interaction during the eating and drinking, and it is also a decent and reasonable thing to do, and is likely to be perceived like that.

### Engaging victims

For youth justice Conferences, there is a fundamental issue of engaging victims. This, of course, needs as much sensitivity and care as the work with offenders and their families. Victims may be reluctant to attend, and concern about revictimisation must be paramount. Again the emphasis of the work should be on providing support for attendance, rather than alternative means of representation, but if absolutely necessary it is possible to put victim's views to Conferences on paper or via others. Supporters may have a key role, preferably within the victim's own family, but possibly via friends or via professionals such as victim support schemes. The effect on the victim is central, but it is their absolute right to refuse to attend if that is really what they wish.

Corporate victims, such as stores, need to be represented by an individual who was affected; the human exchange between the victim and the offender is a key part of the Conference, and all crimes have some impact on the people involved, even when they concern theft from shops. Multiple victims, for example of a series of car crimes, may elect to have a representative for a number of them, but this should be their decision not the co-ordinator's.

As the victim is a central element of the Conference the place and style of the Conference should be fully acceptable to them, and discussing this with them both emphasises their importance, and makes it more likely that they will attend.

## Practicalities

The venue and a whole range of practical details are very important. Making sure that transport is possible, or that child care is available, may particularly affect attendance when there is already some reluctance to go.

Neutral venues are likely to be better than ones associated directly with the services involved (for example the social services' office) or with particular elements of the family (for example a grandmother's house). A former staff flat attached to a children's home may be a practical solution, as it would also provide facilities for food, and more than one room. It is also likely to have ground floor access, probably suitable for those who have a disability.

Having at least two rooms is important, and it is preferable to have three: to greet different groups, to provide a waiting room during private family time and to provide a possible room for people, perhaps especially children, to retire to if the proceedings are getting too much, or in the case of young children when the proceedings are getting too boring.

The timing of the meeting needs to be convenient for the family. The language of the meeting needs to be that preferred by the family, and ideally the co-ordinator should be able to speak that language. Interpreters may of course be necessary, and if any of the professionals cannot speak the chosen language then interpreters should be used, rather than relying on the co-ordinator's language skills if they have them, in order to avoid any compromise of the co-ordinator's role.

## Clear information

The Conference should begin with a statement about the purpose from the co-ordinator, or possibly from the young person or a key family member if that is the style of this particular Conference. Process and ground rules should always be covered by the co-ordinator, stressing during this that information should be confidential to the Conference. The information sharing stage should always begin with a contribution from a key family member, even if it is very brief at this point.

Ideally written information, in the form of reports, should be available to the family in the chosen language and, as discussed above, ideally there will be no new news in such reports. The availability of flip charts, marker boards, paper and pens may be helpful to the family to make notes in the light, or the absence, of such reports. Sensitivity to literacy abilities may of course be needed.

The success or failure of the Conference will be built on the quality of the information that is given in the first session. Co-ordinators should do their best to ensure that reports are clear and jargon-free, and during the meeting they must be completely confident that all relevant information has been covered and understood: the purpose of this first stage of the Conference is to provide the information that is needed to enable the family to plan. Being sensitive to the wide range of jargon that is an inevitable feature of professional life is central to this role.

Alongside clear information about the problems, there should be clear information about relevant services that are possibly available.

## Chairing the meeting

The family should be the first to enter the room in which the Conference will take place, except for youth justice where the victim and their family or supporters should be the first. The seating can be arranged as they want, and the professionals then follow.

The purpose of the meeting should have been discussed with all participants beforehand. The outline of the Conference and its purpose should be covered, as mentioned above, and everyone should introduce themselves.

Constant attention is required to the dynamics of the group and the interaction of the members of the Conference.

A flip chart, or a large sheet of paper on the wall, is useful to note different stages of the Conference on. It keeps the structure clearly in everyone's minds. When moving to the family session it is useful to record the main issues to be addressed on such a sheet, and to leave this with the family. Presenting these main issues also continues to reinforce the message that the focus of the meeting is on the welfare of the child. In the last stage of the meeting a large sheet or flip chart may also be helpful to record the points that are agreed.

### Police and co-ordinator roles

For youth justice Conferences the opening needs to follow a rather different pattern to that outlined earlier, which will involve the police statement, the offender's response to these facts and the victim's commentary on the effects. The Conference is centred around the victim and speed is likely to be encouraged in the private session to avoid leaving the victim waiting for too long.

## Moving to the family session

The co-ordinator needs to have a discussion with the family members which includes checking that:

- Every professional present is confident that they have conveyed all the relevant information to the family
- Every family member feels that they have asked all the questions they wish to ask
- Information about possible services has been given
- Key issues to be addressed in the family's private time are clear

A statement to move on could be something like:

> 'We can now go on to the family decision making part of the meeting. I would like to remind you that we are here to help with $x$ and $y$ issues, about this young person, and to decide the actions that need to be taken about them. What we will be looking for is a plan that is agreed by everyone, with contributions from all as they wish, and that asks for all the services that you think may be useful, which of course may be different from those we have

mentioned. We will try to be as helpful as we can. We will be around to help you, if you wish. Any plan will need to have a review built into it and suggestions of what to do if things go wrong.'

### And to the victim session

The private family time is also a chance for the victim and their family/supporters to have some private time, or to meet with the co-ordinator away from the offender and their family. Issues that they did not want to cover with the offender present can be discussed and, for some, fears and anxieties can be addressed. Occasionally there will be issues raised which the co-ordinator will bear in mind at the final agreement stage, and that they will introduce themselves on behalf of the victim, although they may not mention that it is the victim's concerns they are raising. For example a victim may be very concerned that they do not have to see the offender during some reparation tasks which look likely to be agreed, and the co-ordinator may then be willing to make sure that the timing of such tasks is agreed appropriately during the final session.

## Practising respect

Overall the Conference approach is designed to be as respectful as possible of family heritage and culture, within the clear limits of the law, for example regarding racist provocation. This is implicit in much of the guidance above.

The recruitment of co-ordinators should consider the race, culture, religion and language of the populations they are serving. The venues available should equally pay such attention, and be appropriate for the families concerned.

There may need to be particular attention paid to the fact that some family members counter the discrimination they experience in everyday life by a variety of covert means, and due respect should be given to this. For example those who are in gay/lesbian relationships and who do not wish to *come out* at this stage.

Co-ordinators will almost certainly be uncomfortable with some aspects of family behaviour, and find some family interactions not to their liking. They should encourage decent behaviour, and they should firmly oppose behaviour which could be against equal opportunities or race relations legislation, but within these boundaries respecting the family's own way of working is vital. Co-ordinators should treat families with respect, and not impose their own views.

It is also crucial to be aware that the use of a respectful model of decision-making does not guarantee respectful services!

## Dealing with the unexpected

Each Conference will be unique, and will generate a range of difficult decisions for co-ordinators, and for family members and professionals. How should co-ordinators handle the unexpected? There are some possible guidelines, but of course by its very nature the unexpected cannot be fully accounted for in advance. Suitable strategies could include:

- Reminding everyone that the child's welfare is the priority
- Naming and facing up to problems
- Providing a break to allow things to calm down
- Asking for family strategies to resolve difficulties
- Making sure that those who leave the meeting unexpectedly can find somewhere to go that may allow them to rejoin at a suitable time

## Clarifying agreements

The meeting should begin with clear information and, assuming all has gone well, end with clear agreements. To achieve this co-ordinators must play an active role in clarifying exactly who is agreeing what. There is a fine line between clarifying and changing! Questions about who, what, when, how and why may aid the process of clarification, but they can also form a subtle way to convert family views towards professional views. If professional views clash with family ones at this stage then this should be explicit and not implicit.

The purpose of clarification is to make sure that the family is clear, and then on the basis of that clarification to make sure that the professionals are satisfied. Some renegotiation may be needed, and some further clarification.

An option to bear in mind is that the family can always meet again to clarify issues, perhaps briefly now, or maybe reconvening, although time passing by may not be acceptable. It is possible for the family to nominate a smaller group of people who will be responsible for some further negotiation outside the Conference.

Co-ordinators may consider joining the family when they have finished their private time, and before the professionals are invited back, in order to review any issues that may need clarification, and perhaps suggest a little extra private family time to do this.

When the family is joined again by the professionals, and the plan is presented and discussed, it is the job of the professionals and not the co-ordinator to decide if the plan poses a risk of significant harm to the child. In practice the vast majority of plans do not. But the co-ordinator needs to be very clear that they are not responsible for either family or professional judgements at this stage – they are responsible for making sure that both sets of judgements are being made properly and are being expressed clearly.

*Youth justice*

This final stage will be similar to the child welfare one, but the agreement will need to consider how far the suggestions proposed put things right, probably by having some element of reparation, alongside some penalties. There must be a professional judgement as to how appropriate the proposals are for the offence committed; are they, for example, far too harsh or far too lenient. They may need to be acceptable to a court. The victim must be fully involved and there may be, as mentioned earlier, some information from the victim that has been given privately to the co-ordinator, which needs to play a role in shaping the final agreement. Clarifying the different elements of all this is a substantial task for co-ordinators.

## Monitoring

After the Conference there needs to be some monitoring of the plans that are made, which should be agreed as part of the plans themselves. The monitoring may be via the family, or a social worker, or both. Any party has the right to call another Conference if they wish, and the co-ordinator needs to emphasise this. Monitoring involves checking on the plan, seeing whether or not services that were promised have been available and whether or not family ideas were followed. It is not a social work assessment, although it is possible that such an assessment was built into the plan. Monitoring is a very important responsibility.

## Conclusions

Family Group Conferences, initially developed in New Zealand, provide a way to add to the information regarding the seriousness of issues, to engage more family in the debate and to seek agreement, and therefore concerted action, on behalf of the welfare of a child or young person. They build on the practical and psychological strengths and importance of the family. They are based on jargon-free information, a wide concept of family, independent co-ordinators, respect for family views and a focus on family strengths. In the case of youth justice they have a central role for the victim. They are different from many other forms of meetings, and may look very different for different families with different issues in different contexts. They rely on a set of principles, but also recognise that there must at times be pragmatism. Conferences are the art of the possible. They have a sense of occasion, a sense of human frailty and an extraordinary mix of the comic and the tragic, which is somewhat akin to a theatrical performance. Able and skilled co-ordinators are required to run them, and their work is both difficult and intense.

The key elements of the Conference, and the enactment of the Rough Guide to co-ordinating Family Group Conferences, were established in the UK programme by training, meetings, policy development, guidance and other means. This implementation is the subject of the next chapter.

# Chapter 4

# Establishing Family Group Conferences

The focus of this chapter is on how interest in the Family Group Conference model translated into practical action. We follow the *implementation process* from the development of individual interest into a project with staff's policies and procedures. Our understanding of this stage comes from project records such as steering group minutes, interviews over 2 years with the project initiators, experience of input to training and from questions put to the social workers – asking them, for example, for their advice about setting up similar projects in the light of their experience with this one. We also look at the groups of people participating in the project: what sort of families with what sorts of problems had a Family Group Conference? How did social workers engage with the project? What sort of people became co-ordinators and how?

## Implementation in child welfare

As we have discussed in Chapter 1, training events, literature and meetings inspired by the New Zealand example, largely organised by the Family Rights Group, played a key role in creating interest in the model nationally. The interest led a group of individuals to form the pilot project group in 1992, meeting quarterly to discuss the process and practicalities of implementation. Each of the agencies involved was committed to conducting an evaluation of their work, and the appointed researchers formed a second group, the project evaluation group, co-ordinated from the University of Sheffield.

The pilot project group, and the evaluation group, involved teams in six key agencies: five social services departments and one voluntary agency. As noted earlier only four went on to develop the use of Family Group Conferences within the time frame of the research. Therefore, we have information on *project implementation*, which will be discussed in this chapter, from six agencies, and information from four agencies for the later discussions of the *process and outcomes of Family Group Conferences*.

## The early stages

All of the projects developed from the particular interest and enthusiasm of one or two individuals. These people were self selected in that they had obtained funding at their own request to attend training events run by the Family Rights Group. Following training the individuals spoke to others whom they thought would be similarly interested and enthusiastic, gathering together a group of people to take the idea forward within their organisation.

### Individual commitment

In each project, the continuing enthusiasm of individual people for the Family Group Conference model was necessary for the success of the project implementation. The initiators had put a great deal of personal time and effort into the projects, whether they were in practitioner or management level posts. They all said that the encouragement and support of the national pilot project group had been vital to maintain their enthusiasm and determination in the light of the difficulties they faced.

A number of the social workers interviewed recognised the commitment of these individuals and cited the importance for any project of having committed and enthusiastic people within the team:

'I think you have got to be extremely determined and know that you will have to spend a lot of your own time doing it.'

### A project manager?

A number of people suggested that the ideal would be to appoint a project manager, someone with time allocated for consulting with social services staff and other agencies, for co-ordinating the training, negotiating the policies and procedures and keeping the project high on the agenda at every level. In many ways this would solve the difficulties faced by personnel trying to do the project work alongside their normal job. It would also enable issues such as record keeping and evaluation to be addressed more thoroughly. There are however drawbacks, and the experience of the projects we looked at suggests that the project manager route may not always be the most successful, at least in the early stages of implementation.

The level of personal commitment and personal investment seemed to matter a great deal in getting these projects off the ground, and there are hints from the research that *insiders* have a greater understanding of their system and are more able to influence colleagues. The only project that did employ a manager right at the start, St Basils, found major problems in maintaining momentum when the post holder left and there was a gap before a replacement appointment was made. As one of the staff in the pilot programme said:

'I think we could have introduced somebody into the process, a kind of co-ordinating manager long ago. [But] in some ways the project developed out of one person's particular interest and it's needed the fact that one person has had a very big interest in it to keep the impetus going. So I can assume that introducing it cold – if you are really trying to take it on in the one place and let it grow – you almost need somebody's burning ambition to do it, and even a project manager isn't going to make people [do it].'

Using an insider of course has drawbacks in other ways. For example, the initiator in some projects had little or no time allocated to the task. In addition they brought their personal history with that agency to the work, with all the pluses and minuses this might entail. Nonetheless it was clear that strong personal commitment and drive was needed to establish these pilots, and that insiders seemed well placed to use this to best effect.

*Steering group and resources*

Individual commitment to the project appeared to be vital to get it going, but the project's development and form was influenced by interagency commitment. Thus the course of each project was to some extent dictated by the political, financial and social power wielded by the membership of their steering group. Where the managerial commitment had led to a steering group that included senior social work managers and representatives of other agencies (for example one included nurse advisor, county solicitor, police representative and education welfare manager) the project was more assured of financial support and a higher profile in the area. Where the steering group was small and located mainly within the social work team (for example one project had a group of four, three of whom were team members) the project was likely to struggle for resources and recognition.

Again some of the social workers interviewed recognised the importance of gaining influential support, and thus resources. The allocation of resources, helpful in its own right, is probably also perceived as indicative of *serious* backing from on high. As one social worker put it:

'I mean there's no resources! No resources have been provided by the department, there's no commitment from the top to this. They probably think "oh, well done" but they haven't provided the resources.'

Due to the differing sources of support, the projects we studied were able to muster substantially different amounts of both time and money to get started. This would have an effect on the status and momentum of the project. However, the matter of resources is not a straight-forward one. Where resources were allocated, practitioners who did not approve of the project were disgruntled about the 'preferential treatment' given to the project and the allocation of money 'which ought to be used for other things'.

*Involving social work staff in the implementation process*

Social workers' attitudes to the project and the model were affected by the early implementation process. There were a few who complained about the way the project was introduced. These were mostly from the two projects where the initiator was a manager rather than a practi-tioner:

'One of the criticisms we all have is that a memo arrives on your desk saying that this is happening and I think it would be important not to do it that way. If people are going to own it and feel they can use it they need to be part of the discussion in setting it up ... there was a certain amount of prejudice against it I think.'

But even where the initiator was within the social work team, some resistance to the model stemmed from the perceived lack of consulta-tion and involvement from the beginning:

'For a while it didn't feel as if we were really involved, the rest of us staff. I do think it's important to keep the rest of the staff involved and aware and continually given information about what is going on. Otherwise they become resentful, or maybe that's just me.'

We should point out that the project initiators themselves felt they *had* consulted widely, and had been careful not to just *land* the project on people. The perceptions of practitioners might therefore reflect the degree of sensitivity surrounding the Family Group Conference model rather than the reality of the implementation process. What is clear is that implementing Family Group Conferences is not a simple matter of telling people what to do. Everyone we spoke to agreed that the most important part of introducing the Conference model was gaining people's commitment and belief in the model as a different way of working with families. As one said:

'the crucial thing is to capture the imagination of the workers because we suffer, like lots of people, from being told to do all sort of things from the top down. People feel upset, insulted, overworked, over-burdened, because it's just more things we are being told to do and unless people can actually see the sense in it, can see something in it for them, which could be an improvement in practice that's actually possible, then I think social workers will have a thousand and one ways of sabotaging. They just won't refer, they won't do it, they

don't fill in the form, they don't whatever. So you've got to harness
the enthusiasm of the people who are going to start the work off.
Selling it to the troops is the key point.'

This brings us to a consideration of the matter at the heart of implementation – the debates about the model itself, and the process of
'selling it to the troops'.

## The debates

Although managerial support and resources are clearly important in
any new initiative, the more important, and in this case more challenging, task was to develop an understanding of the model amongst the
practitioners being asked to implement it. Without resources the project would struggle, but without referrals and information givers it
would simply not function at all. Much of the personal time and effort
put in by the project initiators centred round explaining, debating and
developing the principles and practice of the Family Group Conference
model with the team members.

We were given an idea of the uphill struggle facing the projects in this
task when one social worker described how she had first heard of the
model at a meeting with other social workers: they had laughed the idea
out of court, dismissing it as 'completely barmy'.

The project initiators found vehement opposition to the model from
a few, and disquiet amongst many others. Once the debate about
Family Group Conferences had begun, it spread to a wider debate
about working with families, about power and about meeting the needs
of children and families. It raised issues about current practice and
procedure, about what is in the best interests of the child, and about
safety and significant harm. The model was not 'just another way of
working', for many it was a challenge to the assumptions underlying
their work, which despite the emphasis on partnership, still revolved
around ideas of professional control, and of families or households
predominantly having 'problems without strengths'.

The social workers, when questioned, were almost all of the opinion
that the opportunity for debate was the most vital aspect of introducing
the Family Group Conference model into practice.

'You will not get anywhere with this until you start addressing
people's attitudes about how they work with families ... giving
people a lot of time to assimilate the ideas, giving people the
opportunities to really explore the anxieties is essential.'

### Other agencies

At the same time as 'selling' the model to social worker practitioners,
the project initiators had to sell it to their managers, to the Area Child

Protection Committee (ACPC) and to other agencies. In as much as other professionals would be expected to be information givers, they needed to be alerted to the expectations and implications of the model as it affected them. This work went on at different levels in different projects. Contact with other agencies through the steering group or the ACPC was thought to help 'spread the word'. In addition, project initiators tried to arrange meetings with groups of whoever they thought relevant, and spent a lot of time talking about the model around their district. For instance, one project initiator gave presentations to the Area Health Authority, the District Review co-ordinator, the Social Services Committee and Children's Subcommittee, the District ACPC and the District Review Committees. In another area, training days were held for the police and for health visitors. As with discussions with the social workers, these meetings could be very difficult. Scorn could be poured on the model: the 'families would never be able to do that' response; or people dismissed the model as nothing different: the 'we Do All That Already' (DATA) response (Marsh, 1990).

## Negotiating policy and procedure

Alongside the work of 'gaining the hearts and minds' of practitioners, as one social worker put it, there is the need to establish a place for the model in existing policy and procedure. This part of the implementation process required project initiators to negotiate with senior managers and representatives of other agencies involved in child welfare work. Much of this work took place at the steering group meetings. As might be expected child protection issues were very prominent in the discussions, and negotiations with the ACPC and any relevant subcommittees were necessary. Again, these discussions could sometimes be difficult, with the differing cultures and customs of agencies exposed as they discussed their reaction to the innovative Conference model.

### Child protection

Child protection is clearly a fraught and delicate area. Examples from two of the projects will give a flavour of the issues that the projects faced in trying to introduce the Conferences into this area of work.

The Winchester project sought to hold Family Group Conferences prior to initial child protection conferences, so that the family plan could be presented at this conference for acceptance. This would have meant getting agreement to extend somewhat the length of time before the child protection conference. Although there was support for this proposal from many ACPC members, the police objected on a number of counts, imposing a number of restrictions on the type of case that could use Family Group Conferences in this way. Development then had to proceed at a much slower pace.

In Gwynedd one trigger for referral to the project was to be registration at the initial child protection conference. It was assumed that registration would be based on clear criteria of risk, which could then be the basis of the issues given to the family to be resolved or addressed at the Family Group Conference. It was quickly realised that the initial conference was not always so clear about the nature of risk. The project therefore raised awkward questions for established procedures, ruffling a few feathers in the process.

The projects therefore took the view, or at least came round to the view, that negotiating an innovative place for the model in child protection procedures, such as replacement of the child protection conference, was too demanding a task. A number of factors seemed to be involved in this decision:

- Resistance to the model from some quarters were such as to indicate the effort would be wasted.
- The pilot project was small and it did not initially warrant the upheaval involved with changing existing procedures.
- Negotiating to change procedures required senior manager status or support which was not always available.
- Child protection procedures have a high status and profile, and suggesting changes to them would prolong the implementation, and might even jeopardise the whole project.
- Child protection work is often the more complex and difficult, so it might be more appropriate to *prove* the model on the more straightforward cases first.

Most projects started off focusing on accommodated children and requests for accommodation, and cases where care proceedings were being considered or initiated. The projects then moved on to either increasing or including child protection work once experience and confidence in the model had been established.

As noted before, attempts to hold Family Group Conferences prior to child protection conferences became mired in difficulties. Most projects were proposing that the Conference be held after the initial child protection conference. It was envisioned that sometimes the decision to register might be deferred until after consideration of the Conference plans. More usually the Family Group Conference would take place after registration, and the effects of the Conference plans would be considered at a review conference. All those that did include child protection work added the caveat that sexual abuse cases would be excluded at least to begin with, the exception being the Leamington Spa project, but work here failed to get off the ground in any substantial manner. In practice sexual abuse cases were referred to the projects and are included in this study.

## Referrals criteria

The local factors within the area social services departments and interagency systems led each project to develop slightly different referral criteria. In one, referral was to be automatic for two groups of children: where accommodation was being requested or had already happened but plans were needed, and following new child protection registrations. In other projects, the referral to the project from the groups identified was a matter of choice for the social worker. Even within this, the projects differed widely. In one project referral was expected from social workers 'interested in the method' wanting to use the model instead of planning meetings for children in need, and the emphasis was on working with families who were 'accessible and willing to engage'. In another, social workers were strongly encouraged to refer to the project, with each new case being considered for referral as it came in for allocation. In these cases, once referral was agreed it was expected that the co-ordinator would visit the family regardless of how willing or accessible they might initially appear.

The projects were therefore placing different demands upon their social workers and co-ordinators. They did, however, all have well thought out documents stating the policy of the project, and the procedures to be used.

## Referral procedure

Once social workers had decided to refer to the project, often following discussion with team leaders and with project staff, there was a referral form to fill in. This usually required basic information about the child, their family and the reason for the referral. One project form asked the social worker to provide a family tree, which was found to be helpful to the co-ordinators. Others elicited comments on the preferred race or gender of the co-ordinator.

The referral form would usually then go to a project panel for discussion, the panel consisting of the project manager/initiator(s) and team leaders. If the panel agreed that it was appropriate to try to hold a Conference, a co-ordinator would be allocated to the family.

## Information leaflets

Each project prepared an information leaflet for families. The content of each is similar, focusing on what a Family Group Conference is and how it works, and answering basic questions about the model, including who might attend, what might happen about disagreement and what should happen after the Conference. In Leamington Spa a short version was printed in English and Punjabi and in North Wales the leaflet was in English and Welsh. Each had space for the co-ordinator's name and contact number and the social worker's name.

## Recruiting the co-ordinators

Three of the projects had negotiated agreement to recruit external co-ordinators, and so this was the next task for the project organisers. The numbers recruited and becoming active in the role varied considerably: in Winchester it was ten, in Wandsworth six and in Gwynedd two people covered all the work in the first 2 years, with more being recruited later.

Almost all of the co-ordinators we spoke to had been recruited by word of mouth rather than through advertisement. In one project, a large multidisciplinary meeting to explain the project ended with a request for anyone interested in the co-ordinator role to get in touch and this led to significant interest. These were among the co-ordinators who said 'I heard about it and got interested'. In other projects, staff involved mentioned the project to friends and colleagues who they thought might be interested. This group, around half, said 'someone suggested it to me'. In this way potential co-ordinators were recruited from amongst the local statutory and voluntary service communities, and then were interviewed and appointed in the usual manner.

### Co-ordinator background

It is not surprising that many of the co-ordinators had a social work background. Three quarters of them had a social work qualification, and just over half had experience in a social services area team, just over one in ten had experience in probation, and slightly less than one in ten had experience in education welfare. In addition quite a high proportion, just over a third, had experience of a teaching or training role.

Other background experience included community worker, counsellor, foster carer, refuge worker, youth worker, nursing and parenthood. Only one had no work experience in the caring services sector, but was recruited from a local authority research team.

Job descriptions were drawn up by some of the projects after much debate, but to some extent these were a shot in the dark because the relative importance of different skills was not known. In reality it seems that people suggesting themselves were usually taken on for training to see if they fitted the role. In each of the projects one or two co-ordinators were recruited who did not go on to undertake the task – some because their other work demands did not allow the time, others because of the complexities of the role.

### Pay and conditions

The co-ordinators' employment status and pay varied from project to project. Two projects had funds to pay their co-ordinators. Both decided to set a *per conference* payment, based roughly on the average hours work expected, and the guardian *ad litem* rates of pay, the agreed sum being around £350. This *flat rate* payment has recently been under review because of the wide range in hours taken on the task and the possibility that the co-ordinators will be tempted to *cut corners* to reduce the time taken. The issue of costs is returned to in Chapter 9.

Where the co-ordinators were already in employment, there was usually an agreement for them to take on the role where they could fit it in with their normal work, and the agency would benefit from the fee. In Wandsworth, where funds were not available, the co-ordinators were recruited from within other teams or sections of the social services department. No money changed hands and the co-ordinators negotiated to undertake the role in work time. Fitting in the unpredictable co-ordinator role with other work, whether salaried or freelance, occasionally caused considerable stress, and one co-ordinator withdrew from the role because of this.

## Training

Training played a central role in the development and the implementation of the Family Group Conference programme. As we have discussed in Chapter 1 the initial impetus for much of the work came from the courses run by Family Rights Group in 1994 and 1995. The projects themselves then developed training for the staff involved, and particularly for the co-ordinators. We could only gather retrospective information and opinion about the training programmes that each project used within the social work teams and with multiagency representatives. Asking people to cast their minds back to training some months earlier proved an insurmountable stumbling block: memories were scant and opinions bland. We were therefore unable to obtain much information regarding the participants' views of training; it was undoubtedly the case that there was much support for the training, but detailed reflection on it was not available. However, the overall views did indicate a theme, touched on towards the start of this chapter, which is of great importance in this area: the need for training to be linked firmly to ideals and principles.

> 'Massive amounts of training are needed because it is an attitudinal shift, you are not just saying "this is our new procedure, you must follow it", there needs to be some commitment in the people to the idea of working with the strengths in families and the beliefs in families.'

We will return to this theme shortly.

### *The training in the projects*

A general, and brief, introduction to the project was usually offered to a wide range of staff who might come into contact with the programme, with more time being given to those who are more centrally involved.

Substantial training efforts were focused on co-ordinators. Many had attended the Family Rights Group training days, although sometimes after they had had experience of co-ordinating. In one area the co-ordinators met as a group for training days and sessions spaced over the year before the project was launched. This was described as 'partly exploring, partly training', 'exploring the issues with lengthy role plays', and 'going over things from your own life'. In other areas training was more ad hoc, with plans for an inexperienced co-ordinator to shadow a more experienced one not always coming to fruition, and 'learning as you go' sometimes being preferred. This approach was described as 'generating practice from principles', and in so far as it was genuinely reflecting on principles it appeared to work better than some might have expected. It may have gone some way towards making sure that the ideals and philosophy *were* the driving forces behind the work.

Generally speaking social workers were asked to attend a training day at which the model was introduced from an historical perspective, and the process explained. Further training, for example on two separate days, was then arranged at a later date, to discuss the implications of the model in practice.

Between each training event, the model was discussed informally, sometimes it seems in quite a heated manner, amongst the team members. The opportunity for team discussion was described as very important, and it was clearly dependent on having someone in the team conversant and committed to the model to engage in the debates:

> 'It's certainly been useful for us to have somebody in the team as a practitioner who has been setting it up as opposed to something that's been brought in from sideways or above, because the debate is constantly open and things are changing.'

Introducing Family Group Conferences required a great deal of diligent effort and continuing discussion.

## Introducing a 'different way of working'

As the programmes developed so the training developed, and with the addition of new projects in Haringey and in Wiltshire, a model of training evolved which built on the best features in each of the separate projects. The context, within social services, was of the widespread continuing difficulties in linking any new policies and practices with relevant training, a situation that was perhaps especially true when the changes involved *empowering* models of work.

The difficulties of introducing different ways of working had been highlighted with the introduction of the new Community Care programme in the UK in the early 1990s. The importance of linking policy and practice development with training was stressed very strongly in guidance for the new Act, and there were explicit exhortations to make such links (Social Services Inspectorate, 1991: p. 109). However in a survey of heads of training carried out some 3 years later this linkage was still regarded as being a major problem (Rai, 1994: p. 44). In connection with empowerment practice, as Stevenson and Parsloe (1993: p. 11) have pointed out, there is a need for managers to model some of the empowerment ideals in their day to day work, but recent changes, policies and structures have not always achieved this. Making the strategic links between management, practitioner and trainer were therefore always likely to be problematic when introducing the empowering Family Group Conference programme. This was borne out by the experience of these projects: implementation time scales grew, and managerial and practitioner support was often patchy out-side of the immediate staff involved.

Lessons from the implementation of the Children Act 1989 were equally relevant. The training required for the Conferences mirrored some of that needed for the development of partnership under the Act (see for example Marsh & Fisher, 1992; Smale *et al.*, 1993). It included the need, as already mentioned, to build the work on a foundation of firm principles, and to encourage managers and practitioners to work together to achieve change. As a partnership training pack puts it, 'this programme will only be fully effective if trainers, managers and staff give an explicit commitment to the ideals put forward and provide each other with as much help as they can to put these ideals into practice' (Newton & Marsh, 1993: p. 11).

The most recent format of the Family Group Conference training programme is outlined below in a Rough Guide to training. In common with the earlier Rough Guide to co-ordinating, it is written as a set of *guidelines*. Details of the sessions and materials involved are contained in a training pack available from Family Rights Group (Morris & Marsh, in press).

## A Rough Guide to training for Family Group Conferences

The training for the staff in the projects was developed and refined a number of times using the experiences of families, social workers and co-ordinators. It addressed three groups of staff: the wide group of staff who might have some connection with the project and therefore needed to understand the overall Conference process, those who were engaged in assessment and referral and were potentially going to give infor-mation to the Conferences and finally the co-ordinators who were to run the Conferences. The needs of these groups, covering general information, the skills needed to participate and the skills needed to run the Conferences, formed three separate training elements. All relevant staff would need to cover the first area, a more limited number would need to cover the second as well and co-ordinators would need to be well versed in all three.

## Staff who need to understand the Family Group Conference

Many staff will come into contact with the Conferences, and will perhaps need to explain them to others, or respond to aspects of their workings.

A whole range of staff were involved at this stage of the training: reception staff, managers of teams of social workers outside of child care, staff in other children's services and in education and health. Around a half day on the background, philosophy and key practical details is needed to keep them informed. Even at this level of the training two key factors need emphasising. First that the training demonstrates a clear commitment by managers to this way of working, and to supporting staff in undertaking the work. This needs a practical component to show that it is more than just a routine acceptance – perhaps a presentation during the training or an offer of regular review meetings with staff. Second the basic ideals of the model need to be clearly articulated, and any misgivings that staff have about these should be carefully explored.

This is also the starting point for the co-ordinators to be making links with practice and management staff, and if they come from outside the mainstream social services area, to be asking questions about local policies and procedures. The overall theme is that the endeavour will only work if all concerned pull together and operate in partnership, one with another, as well as working in partnership with children and families.

## Staff who will give information to the Conferences

A longer training period, around 2 days, is needed to ensure that the necessary skills for giving information to the Conference are at least explored, and at best enhanced. Again there needs to be serious work on the ideals lying behind the model, and this time, rather than debate some of them, it is best to use one or more exercises which could explore, for example, the way that course members would themselves solve a family problem. When would they turn to social services and when would they want to handle it within their family? If they did turn to social services how would they want to be treated?

There must be a substantial period, at least 1 of the 2 days, practising the actual skills of giving information. Writing in a clear and jargon-free manner does not come easily to most people, and it is even more difficult if there are the inevitable ambiguities and emotional overtones that accompany much of child welfare work. Structuring the day to highlight the benefits that staff can expect to gain from the new model is helpful. Providing some form of role play experience is probably crucial, so that experiment can be undertaken and personal style adapted and developed.

There is an opportunity in the training to involve users, ideally in planning and in presentation (see for example Newton & Marsh, 1993: p. 41), perhaps to suggest the ways in which they would like to be treated, or maybe in describing some aspects of the model from direct experience.

## Co-ordinators

A substantial additional period is needed for training the co-ordinators. They are the linchpin of the work. They will need to have attended all of the previous sessions, but they have a role which is so central, and potentially so difficult, that they must have good detailed training on their own, and continuing follow up in the form of supervision and more advanced training. At this point at least 3 days is needed for the co-ordinators to cover the issues that were sketched out earlier in the Rough Guide to co-ordinating and to work their way from the very beginnings of the Conference process to the final stages of the work.

It is very important to convey the actual experience of a Conference, to try and show the way in which the preparation work is crucial, and how the event itself has a unique life of its own on each occasion. Video may be useful, as may direct user or staff experience. At least 2 of the days will need to be role play, using methods that make sure that all of the relevant elements of the earlier Rough Guide are covered. For example an exercise on identifying family could involve current cases, and the role play could involve staged interruptions that mean decisions need to be taken about exclusion of members, about the use of advocates or about clarifying the meaning of agreed plans.

## On-going training

Providing the basic training is not enough. There needs to be continuing support of the work to make sure that basic principles are being adhered to, and to adapt and develop the work in the light of increased knowledge and local experience. Co-ordinators need support one from another, and also good supervision which will keep them on their toes, keep them relatively unentangled in the depth of the family problems that they deal with and which will check their continuing training needs.

Training is a very important part of the overall work in implementing the projects, but even when it is done very well there is a range of many other managerial tasks and practical details to cover before the first

Conference can be held. Training does not tackle all of the issues necessary to run good Family Group Conferences. It is a necessary but not sufficient condition.

## The projects in action

In this section we return to the pilot programme to consider how the projects got going and who the main groups of participants were. We look at the types of referrals made and the characteristics of the families involved. We also look at the degree of social worker involvement in the projects and at the kinds of people who are thought to be appropriate for the co-ordinator role.

## *Getting going*

The difficulty many social workers and policy makers had in understanding and agreeing the principles of the model meant that introducing Family Group Conferences into practice became a bigger and more time-consuming process than anyone had anticipated. Project initiators were frustrated to find that it took them a year or more to get going, and in the one project that implemented the model within 6 months there was some regret at having 'rushed it'.

Two of the projects, Winchester and Leamington Spa, had launch dates, with presentations and media coverage. Others had less specific start dates, and in Hereford, one of the very first areas to express interest and take action to use the model, three Conferences were held before the project had really been introduced, 'because it seemed to suit...'

In Leamington Spa, there were a few referrals following the launch, most of which did not result in a Conference. The project initiator found that the idea of a family meeting was taken up by families, who met of their own initiative and formulated a plan without the need for a co-ordinator. This was both gratifying and frustrating for those wanting to convene and document a Family Group Conference *proper*. This project was then put on hold because the project initiator did not have the time allocated or available to promote it and work on it. There are now plans, 3 years later, to restart in Leamington.

As noted above, families in Hereford had been offered private time before the project really started: the model here was clearly building on some current practice which had already begun to involve extended family in meetings. The project was thus initiated as a way of extending this practice, and a number of referrals for Family Group Conferences were made and meetings held. However, the project was unable to attract funds for employing independent co-ordinators, despite considerable efforts. The absence of an independent co-ordinator meant that the 'engaging the family members' work was left to the social worker, and the co-ordinator role was limited to chairing the actual Conference. We would speculate that in these circumstances difficult family relationships could not receive the attention they might otherwise have. The project then abandoned attempts to proceed further with the *pure* model, but aimed to incorporate the teams' experience of it into their general practice. The research data collected from the Conferences only included those in the *proper* early stages.

## Rates of referral

Once the projects were launched and ready to go, there was again some frustration on the part of the project organisers because of the slow rate of referrals. Each project in turn got fewer referrals than had been expected, and had to review their evaluation programme along with their expectations. The project initiators reported that the support of the national pilot project group was particularly important for them in the face of these frustrations.

Each project also experienced lulls in referral rates over the years that we looked at. In at least one case this was because of the absence of the project enthusiast from the team over the summer holidays, demonstrating again the need to have someone 'keeping the model on the agenda'.

Not all referrals to the panel were considered appropriate for allocation to a co-ordinator. A few were thought to be unsuitable due to the nature of the case, but more usually allocation was not made because there were plans already in place, or because the family had already indicated their strong resistance to the model. This is similar to information we discuss later, in Chapter 6, relating to cases that were allocated to a co-ordinator but did not in the end result in a Family Group Conference. Although the projects each had slightly different referral procedures, it was rare for any of them to hold more than one or two Family Group Conferences a month over the time of this study.

## What types of cases and families were involved?

As discussed earlier, the projects each had criteria for referrals to be made, concentrating mostly on children at risk of being accommodated or already accommodated. Having gained experience of the model, it became more common for other cases, including child protection cases, to be referred for a Family Group Conference.

Over the period of this research, the reason for referral for the 80 Family Group Conferences studied was recorded by the co-ordinator as shown in Table 4.1.

**Table 4.1** Reasons for referral.

|  | n | % |
|---|---|---|
| Accommodation request/risk | 19 | 23 |
| Placement plan | 20 | 25 |
| Child protection, at home | 18 | 22 |
| Child protection, looked after | 14 | 18 |
| Bereavement/illness plan | 5 | 6 |
| Support plan (learning disability) | 1 | 1 |
| Family support/contact plan | 3 | 4 |

n = number of Family Group Conferences

### Child protection

In all 40% of the meetings related to child protection concerns, and overall 44 children were involved. The categories of concern included sexual abuse as well as neglect and physical and emotional abuse. In Table 4.2 we have compared the categories of concern in our sample of child protection children with those going to child protection conferences (Thoburn *et al.*, 1995: p. 70). It is clear that the Family Group Conference was being used disproportionately more for cases of neglect and less for physical and sexual abuse than would be expected in a sample of children going to initial child protection conferences. However the figures do indicate that the model can and has been used with the full range of concerns.

**Table 4.2** Child protection referrals in the national context.

|  | Neglect (%) | Physical (%) | Emotional (%) | Sexual (%) | Not known (%) |
|---|---|---|---|---|---|
| FGC (n = 44) | 54 | 11 | 9 | 7 | 18 |
| Thoburn *et al.* (1995) (n = 220) | 12 | 45 | 4 | 28 | Grave concern 12 |

n = number of children

We are aware that the category of abuse does not necessarily indicate the level of concern: a case of severe neglect may carry a higher level of concern than a case of 'at risk of sexual abuse'. In the absence of other indicators, we have used the decision to register a child as an approximate measure of level of concern. Comparing the rate of registration in our sample with that found by Thoburn and her colleagues, we find that the Family Group Conference children were raising broadly similar levels of concern (Table 4.3).

**Table 4.3** Registered and non-registered cases in the national context.

|  | Child Protection Conference (%) | Family Group Conference (%) |
|---|---|---|
| Registered | 61 | 64 |
| Not registered | 35 | 33 |
| Decision deferred | 4 | 3 |

### Characteristics of the families

In the pilot projects, therefore, Family Group Conferences have been held for the full range of referrals, and as far as we could ascertain the child protection cases seemed to carry the same broad level of concern as the normal child protection population. However we have to consider the possibility that the families were an easier group to work with by virtue of their social circumstances or other qualities, when compared to the social workers' normal case load. We have considered this from two angles. First we compared our sample with those in other studies, to see if they were different on any significant demographic or social indicators. Second we looked at the views and experiences reported by the social workers.

Bebbington and Miles (1989) identify factors associated with risk of entry into care in their study on the circumstances of 2528 children who entered care during 1987. Thoburn *et al.* (1995) similarly identified factors associated with the calling of an initial child protection conference on 220 children. We asked social workers for information relating to these risk factors on the children for whom Family Group Conferences were held. Our comparative groups of looked after and child protection cases were of 23 and 34 children respectively (see Table 4.4, which has Bebbington and Miles's, and Thoburn and her colleague's, categories; data from both comparative studies).

Whilst our sample groups are small, the data indicate that the children referred for Family Group Conferences have very similar risk factors in their backgrounds. There is nothing here to suggest that these cases are any easier to work with or to solve than others.

### Race

The number of children from ethnic minority groups was 13% overall, and almost all of these were from the inner city project area of Wandsworth. They were mostly described in social services' categories as of Afro-Carribean, black British or mixed parentage, and made up half of the cases held in that project. This means that the 'mixed race' information given to us may include those who are not 'mixed'. It also

**Table 4.4** The families in the national context.

|  | Looked after (%) | Bebbington & Miles (1989) (%) | Child protection (%) | Thoburn et al., (1995) (%) |
|---|---|---|---|---|
| Age <5 | 30 | 30 | 44 | 33 |
| 14–15 | 21 | 23 | | |
| 12+ | | | 16 | 33 |
| Boys | 26 | na | 39 | 44 |
| Girls | 74 | na | 61 | 56 |
| In sibling group | 47 | 38 | 55 | 41 |
| Single adult household | 47 | 45 | 52 | 40 |
| Head of household on supplementary benefit | 84 | 66 | 81 | 64 |
| Mixed race | 30 | 6 | 18 | 6 |
| Crowded house | 26 | 28 | na | na |
| Mum <21 | 10 | 5 | na | na |
| Poor area | 68 | 56 | na | na |
| *n* = | 23 | 2500 | 34 | 220 |

*n* = number of children
na = not available.

suggests that ethnic minority children are over-represented in our 'looked after' group, which probably reflects their over-representation in the looked after population as a whole. There was no difference in outcome of the Family Group Conferences for any of the different heritage groupings.

There were concerns in Wandsworth that the project might not be acceptable to the black population because of the social services department being 'seen as a white organisation'. There was no evidence that the Afro-Carribean, black British or mixed parentage families were less likely to use the project than white families, but it may be that families with other origins such as Moroccan, Turkish or Asian found it more difficult. The issue of race in the use of Family Group Conferences in the UK is being looked at in more detail in the Haringey project currently under way as part of the 'Pulling Together' programme (see Chapter 5).

### Previous contact with social services

All but 11 of the families had had contact with the social services department about the child concerned prior to the referral for a Family Group Conference, many of them being known to services for a long time. Four others were known because of the mothers' or siblings' history with social services; only seven families were completely new referrals.

### Separation and divorce

In two thirds of the families involved the parents were separated, and at least a third of the children had experience of one or more step-parents or cohabitee-parents.

### 'Easy' families?

Social risk factors aside, some cases are likely to be easier to work with by virtue of the personalities involved. We were interested to know if social workers referred families to the project because they could be expected to work cooperatively with the model or whether perhaps they referred their most difficult cases in the hope that they might be solved. We found some evidence for both factors.

One research report (Thomas, 1994) found that the model was used 'when other methods had failed', and several social workers spoke to us of using the model when 'stuck' or having 'run out of ideas'. The high incidence of families well known to the social services would support this use of the project. At the same time there was a tendency to refer families who were thought to be 'accessible and willing', particularly at the start of the projects when all the staff involved were on a steep learning curve.

When all the social workers were asked how they would select families for referral to Family Group Conference, only 21% suggested reasons for *excluding* cases on the basis of the type of problem, such as those involving complex child protection issues. That is, the majority would not necessarily exclude a family because of the nature of the case. They are more likely to take into consideration their knowledge or judgement of the family. Almost half (48%) mentioned criteria to do with their knowledge of the size of the family, such as 'when I know there is extended family'. Others would make a judgment on the family's ability 'to formulate a plan' or 'pull together' before referring.

However, of the social workers who had actually been to a Conference just over half, including some from each project, said they had been surprised by the outcome. That is, although they had referred a family to the project, social workers often had considerable doubts about the family's ability to use the Conference productively. Typical comments were:

'We actually did get people into the same room having a fairly amicable discussion, which given the various things that had happened previously was quite a surprise.'

'I think the expectation of the meeting was that it was likely to be very aggressive and very violent, but in actual fact it wasn't at all. That was defused quite quickly and quite easily within that group setting.'

In fact the majority of social workers thought that family responses were not predictable; in total 78% felt they would not be able to predict what their clients would say or do at a Family Group Conference. Those with the greater experience were more likely to comment that families often defied expectations: 'the ones that I thought would develop a plan didn't and those that I didn't, did'.

In addition co-ordinators reported that the social workers often have very limited information on extended family. In their experience, given time a family group can usually be contacted where none was thought to exist, and family members can be brought to work together where disputes or estrangement were thought to make this impossible. Thus, although apparently reasonable, referral criteria that rely on a social worker's judgement of the family's suitability to cooperate and work with the model may exclude families who could make good use of the meeting.

## Social workers' participation

In view of the difficulties each project had experienced in persuading social workers to accept and work with the model, we were interested to know how many had actually engaged in the project. Almost all of the social workers we spoke to gave some indication of appreciating the value of the Family Group Conference model. They saw a difference between the Family Group Conference and other meetings such as child protection conferences and review meetings and they gave almost universally positive answers to the question 'does the Family Group Conference model empower families?' (Table 4.5). The great majority of social workers also wanted the project to continue (Table 4.6). Despite this, over half (55%) of the social workers we spoke to had not

**Table 4.5** Social worker views on Family Group Conferences and 'difference' and 'empowering families'.

|  | Yes (%) | Yes, but (%) | No (%) | Don't know (%) |
|---|---|---|---|---|
| Is the FGC different from other meetings? (n = 62) | 92 | — | 5 | 3 |
| Does the FGC model empower families? (n = 58) | 74 | 26 | 0 | 0 |

n = number of respondents

**Table 4.6** Social worker views on the project continuing.

|  | Increase funding (%) | Keep (%) | Indifferent (%) | Don't know (%) |
| --- | --- | --- | --- | --- |
| What would you like to see happen to the project in the future? | 55 | 19 | 7 | 19 |

attended a Family Group Conference and around a third (31%) had not referred a family to the project at all over 2 years or more of the project operation. This was a common finding in all the participating teams; it was not a case of one project being much more involving of social workers than another. We conclude that, despite expressed positive views, about a third of social workers do not want to use the Conference model.

### Reasons for social workers' non-engagement

A number of different possible reasons for social worker reluctance to use the model, despite their favourable views, have been explored. No significant relationship was found between non participation in the project and length of experience in child and family work. Nor was length of time in the team related to engagement with the project. When we looked at the social workers' length of time in the project team we found that a significant number had joined the team since the initial project training. Half the newcomers had referred to the project and half had not. This seems to suggest that the training did not have much effect on the social workers' willingness to engage with the model: some are attracted to it and some are not.

We did consider the possibility that social workers most dissatisfied with the current systems of working would be those more likely to gravitate towards the Family Group Conference model, and we found some support for this. Social workers were asked their opinions on state care, the importance of family links for children, child protection case conferences and sharing information with families. There was a trend for those most critical of current practice to be more enthusiastic about the new project, but this did not reach significance.

Only a very small number of social workers actually stated that they were opposed to the model. Their answers to an indirect question may give more clues as to why they were reluctant to refer families to the programme. We asked about the overall impact of the model on practitioners: 'what does the model do for social workers generally?'.

- 40% felt it threatened them or reduced their power
- 38% said that it clarified their responsibility and was an aid to partnership
- 22% said that it helped them or made them take a wider view of families

Social workers' feelings about the Family Group Conference model form two sides of the same coin. On the one side the passing of power and responsibility to families is threatening and to be avoided. On the other side the same shift in power is seen as a welcome sharing of responsibility with clearer roles. We are left with the impression that willingness to become involved with the model may be a matter of personality as much as anything else. The factors involved seem to be a complex mix of willingness to engage with new ideas and underlying attitudes as to the nature, meaning and value of *family*.

Although there does seem to be a proportion of social workers who continue to avoid the model, we found evidence that over time people may be persuaded to 'give it a try'. At least some sceptics can be 'brought around'. This means that it was worth the projects keeping it on the agenda, to stimulate further debate. What had been most persuasive for social workers was feedback from users. In one project a user was invited to speak to the area teams and several practitioners spoke of being in tears after hearing her story. In other projects feedback from the researchers seemed effective in improving the referral rate. Opportunities for sharing experiences of the model were also appreciated: one successful outcome can be very powerful. Perhaps the main message here is to keep on 'selling' the model.

## Co-ordinators' contributions

Although the experience of the co-ordinator's role is considered in Chapter 7, we will here look briefly at the contribution the co-ordinators make to the process, in terms of the skills they bring and the practical issues they raise in terms of their support needs and their allocation to families.

### Skills and beliefs

We asked the co-ordinators what skills they thought they had needed. Their replies can be grouped into four broad areas:

- Communication skills:   able to engage people quickly (6)
  listening, clarifying, shaping, interpreting (6)
  negotiation and mediation (7)
- Organisational skills:   co-ordinating information and events (3)
  recording (2)
  word processing (2)

- Specific experience        group work (5)
                             counselling (2)
                             knowledge of the social services (1)
                             theoretical models of child and family
                             work (2)
                             professional networking (3)
- Personal qualities         belief in the model/commitment to the
                             family (6)
                             adaptable and flexible (4)
                             non-interventionalist (4)
                             sense of humour (3)
                             bit of a rebel (2)
                             persistent, creative, imaginative (1 each)

As can be seen, communication skills and personal qualities were those
most often cited as important. The specific skills most often mentioned
were negotiation and mediation, ability to engage people quickly, listening, group work and belief in the model/commitment to the family.
There was little support for the idea that specialist social work skills or
knowledge were very important. Indeed, those who did not have a
social work background felt they were at an advantage in that it
enabled them to see some of the issues more clearly, and avoided the
temptation to 'be a social worker'. Some social worker co-ordinators
agreed that it was difficult to take on the mediator role rather than the
helper role. It was generally felt that experience of working with other
professionals and maintaining clear boundaries, experience of working
with people under stress or in distress, and experience of working with
groups of people, was more important than any particular professional
background.

The importance of belief struck us very strongly in talking to the co-
ordinators:

> 'I think the important thing is that there's a commitment to the
> family, there's a commitment to empowering families.... That
> you're dedicated really, that you're motivated, that you believe in the
> philosophy, that you believe in the model.'

> 'The skill of enabling and really believing in the positiveness of
> empowerment...'

> 'It is about having faith.'

> 'I am constantly satisfied [by the role] by having my inner belief
> confirmed in the fact that people ... do have skills and abilities and
> largely good stuff in them.'

> 'It's about a frame of mind, it's about a belief that families do want
> the best thing...'

'I believe they can change when I go in, I believe they can change the situation, I believe they can see that so I think that's very very important.'

And if the 'belief' is absent, if it is 'just a job'?

'No I don't think you can do it in that respect. I don't think it can work. I think families will know that you are not dedicated, that it's just a job for you.'

The rather *ad hoc* recruitment process was perhaps quite a good way of identifying and appointing people who 'believed' in the model and were willing to learn as they went along.

## Continuing support

All the co-ordinators stressed the need for continuing support and discussion, and spoke highly of the support systems organised. Each project has a co-ordinators group meeting every 3 or 4 weeks for between $1\frac{1}{2}$ hours and 3 hours, facilitated by a project initiator. At this meeting particular cases and issues arising are discussed, so that it acts as a learning forum and support group. In addition to this, co-ordinators will often ring each other up to discuss difficulties. The importance of having somebody available, by telephone or in one to one supervision, to discuss particular crises, was noted by some, and the difficulties of the project initiator taking on a managerial *and* a supervisory role was mentioned by others. However, none doubted the necessity of having regular support meetings.

## Allocation/matching of co-ordinator

In principle attempts are made to match the co-ordinator to the family, based on the family's preference regarding race, gender, language or religion. In the reality of the projects studied here, this was not always practical. Often allocation of a co-ordinator depended on who was available to do the work as much as on who was most appropriate in that instance. However, even where we know of projects making genuine efforts to match co-ordinators to families, the issue is not at all straightforward. This has particularly been the case where co-ordinators have been matched with a family by virtue of their ethnicity. Families may not want to discuss their difficulties with a member of their own community, being concerned that news of their business will travel. They may prefer to have someone who is more obviously distant. At the same time for many black people, racial issues may raise questions about authority and neutrality, such that a white co-ordinator might find their task much more difficult than a black co-ordinator. In the interviews we held with co-ordinators, the issue of race was occasionally mentioned:

'She said to me "well I never knew you were black, if I had known that then I would have made more time to see you".'

In some projects, the issue of language was more pressing. In North Wales, families were always offered the choice of holding the meeting in Welsh or English, and 53% chose Welsh. In other instances, interpreters may be required, and in theory they are there to interpret for the professionals rather than for the family. We have heard accounts of families being able to communicate together and with professionals for the first time, because of the provision of interpreters, sometimes across three languages for different sides of the family. The issues of race and language in Family Group Conferences are being explored in depth in further research (Crow & Marsh, in press; Shepherd, in press).

The question of matching co-ordinators is therefore complex but needs to be addressed, particularly where the client population is multi-ethnic. In the London area, there is a move towards projects setting up a pool of co-ordinators with different backgrounds and languages, to try to meet the needs of the varied population. However, we have learnt that social workers and project managers cannot make assumptions about who a family would prefer. In addition it may be difficult for a family themselves to identify the sort of person they would prefer, for a task that they are unfamiliar with, and projects will have to continue to do the best they can in this difficult area.

## Conclusions

Implementing the Family Group Conference model in social work practice in the UK has, to date, needed considerable commitment and enthusiasm, coupled with the ability to negotiate resources, multi-agency involvement and policy and practice issues. The implementation process needs a considerable amount of time, particularly for training and debate that addresses the attitudes and anxieties of practitioners relating to innovative partnership practice.

Practice has established that the model can be used with the whole range of child welfare concerns, and there is no indication that the pilot projects were concentrating on *easy* cases. Practitioners cannot predict how families will respond to the challenge of the Conferences, and are often surprised at how well things turn out: it seems that almost any family has the potential to benefit.

The model is also a challenge to professionals in that it changes the balance of power, and focuses on the ability of the family to find the resources to meet and make plans. About a third of social workers in each of the teams studied had declined to take up this challenge. In contrast all the people recruited to the role of co-ordinator had in common a belief in partnership practice with families, and in the ability of families to use the model. This, together with communication, group and organisational skills, seemed to define the qualities of a co-ordinator. Specific professional knowledge was thought to be less important.

# Chapter 5

# International Developments and Research

In this chapter we briefly move away from the pilot project to set the UK research programme in the context of the international development and use of Family Group Conferences. We provide a summary of the research studies that have accompanied these developments and outline the results relating to the process, outcomes and participant views. As we shall see, international findings closely echo those described later in this book.

## The international dimension

Family Group Conferences are being developed in many different countries, either within existing legal frameworks, or as part of new ones. There are pilot projects and more mainstream practice developments, limited legal changes and, in the case of New Zealand, a universal legal change to using Family Group Conferences. Within child welfare they are now a key element of the law in New Zealand and are effectively compulsory for all serious welfare and youth justice cases (Hassall, 1996). In Australia they have been regarded, as in the UK, as consistent with the underlying values of the existing child welfare law (Ban & Swain, 1994a). They have also been established within mainstream child care practice, although with the caveat that some are not Conferences with private family time, in Oregon in the USA. Both Oregon in the USA and British Columbia in Canada have drafted legislation for their use. Elsewhere in Canada and the USA (Hardin, 1996; Immarigeon, 1996), as well as in Israel, Norway and Sweden, there are developments that fit the local communities and the relevant legal systems. A number of the projects, as in New Zealand, have been closely involved with, or developed by, indigenous peoples (Longclaws *et al.*, 1996). Within youth justice there are also widespread developments following on from New Zealand. The most comprehensive work has been in Australia (Power, 1996; Wundersitz & Hetzel, 1996); there have been projects in Canada (Longclaws *et al.*, 1996) and legislative proposals in South Africa (Juvenile Justice Drafting Consultancy 1994). Internationally, the full range of child welfare and youth justice work has been covered, via legislation and via specialised projects such as the Newfoundland abuse study and work which is linked directly to indigenous peoples.

As we have noted earlier the development of Family Group Conferences springs from a number of internationally widespread themes within child welfare and youth justice. These have converged to inspire the dramatic development of a new model, as a leading New Zealand legal commentator has put it (Atkin, 1991).

Legislation in child welfare balances rights and responsibilities of children, parents, families and others, aiming to protect and support children in the context of some hotly contested views about 'the family' and 'the child'. It is inevitably contentious. When it also contains within it a radical model of social work, and when it must allow for flexible and creative responses, the legal debates are likely to grow. Where laws have been enacted, in New Zealand for child welfare and youth justice and in Australia for youth justice, these laws have received substantial support (for example the major governmental enquiry in New Zealand: Mason *et al.*, 1992) alongside critical legal analyses (for example Henaghan & Atkin, 1992; Alder & Wundersitz, 1994; Atkin, 1994; Freeman 1994). Accompanying these legal debates there have been many empirical studies of the Conferences. We will first discuss the range of data that has been gathered so far, and then the results of the research, with an eye on its relevance to the UK context.

## The research data

Substantial research studies, and reviews, have taken place in New Zealand, in Australia and in Canada, and in due course more information will be available from work under way in Oregon, Sweden and South Africa and, no doubt, from other places where the Conferences are being developed. The research has covered the process of the Conferences, the staff and family views of the Conferences and the Conference outcomes. We outline below the main research that has been published.

### Studies outside the UK

For many of the international developments it is still early days in terms of research programmes. Oregon, where, as we described earlier, the use of Conferences (Family Unity Meetings) has not always provided for the private family time, has nonetheless recorded reductions in out of family placement of children (Graber, 1991). Following links with the New Zealand work, there has been increased use of private family time, and the programme itself has now become substantial. The use of the Oregon Family Unity Meetings rose from 1000 in 1995 to 2000 in

1996, and it became incorporated into mainstream policy towards the end of that year (T. Keys, personal communication). Apart from information gathered on changes in the use of foster placement, research so far in Oregon has been limited and covers only the way that staff have viewed the new development, which showed general, but not overwhelming, staff support (Hill, 1994). Early results from Sweden also show that there may be resistance from a number of staff to the transfer of power that is involved in the Conferences (K. Sundell, personal communication). In common with the findings in the UK there is clearly a minority of staff who have doubts about the model, a finding which would, of course, probably be true for most practice developments. In South Africa research is currently under way in a child welfare and a youth justice pilot programme (C. Frank, personal communication) focusing in one city on family preservation services and in another on diversion at pretrial stage of young people accused of a range of offending covering about half of the court referrals.

### New Zealand

A major opportunity for policy evaluation occurred in New Zealand with the introduction of the Children, Young Persons and Their Families Act in 1989. Changes in the use of legal options, placements, the use of care and other areas were anticipated and could have been reviewed, if there had been suitable monitoring data before and after the Act. An evaluation could have been carried out against the principles that the Act upholds. At an early stage this was considered, and discussions were held on evaluating the impact of the Act within the Department of Social Welfare (A. Donnell, personal communication), and ideas were canvassed for the recording of data under a new computerised system. Sadly this major opportunity was missed. The computer system was not up to the job, and there were major gaps in the relevant data (Robertson, 1992) over much of the crucial time period: data from before the Act are limited and there are few reliable data in the early years after its introduction. For example there is almost nothing on placement patterns for the years 1990 to 1992, emergency protection figures are sketchy for the period 1987 to 1991 and there are few data on ethnicity of children in the care system for the relevant period. The opportunity was present to monitor a major experiment and provide an internationally relevant evaluation of the new law, practice and policies, but sadly we are left without the benefit this would have given us of detailed and widespread research on these issues.

Despite this lost opportunity for policy evaluation, there was a substantial amount of research undertaken in the early years of the Act. Paterson and Harvey (1991) provided a substantial review of 184 Family Group Conference cases. The work was based on questionnaires to co-ordinators, with 50 of the 54 child welfare co-ordinators responding, along with 142 Family Group Conference plans, and a range of staff interviews. Gilling and her colleagues (1995) provided work on the family views for the same early period, conducting 67 family member interviews from 43 family groups. In this early period there was also a substantial internal review of the working of the Act, which included 82 interviews with staff (Renouf *et al.*, 1990). In the youth justice field Levine and Wyn (1991) interviewed and surveyed youth justice co-ordinators, and Maxwell and Morris (1993) provided a major empirical study of over 200 Family Group Conferences. Finally a major governmental review inquiry (Mason *et al.*, 1992) analysed 350 written submissions as well as 530 oral submissions, attended Family Group Conferences and visited staff and others throughout New Zealand. These early studies provide a wealth of information, but unfortunately they have not been built on, as, at the time of writing, a government commissioned research proposal (Maxwell *et al.*, 1995), designed to pull the work together and provide a sound empirical base for future development, was still not funded.

### Australia

Substantial research on the youth justice developments in Australia has been undertaken (for example Wundersitz & Hetzel, 1996), and the pilot projects in child welfare have also been examined, predominantly within Health and Community Services in Melbourne. Swain (1993) studied 19 Family Group Conferences involving 13 families with 23 children, and interviewed 128 of the Conference participants. Boffa (1995) examined the case data from 42 Family Group Conferences which involved 41 families with 72 children, and Lagay and his colleagues (1994) examined the use of the Conferences as 'prehearing' meetings before court proceedings.

### Canada

In Canada a major developmental research project in Newfoundland (Pennell & Burford, 1995b, 1995c, 1996) has focused on child abuse and domestic violence in three very different cultures. It has covered 37 Family Group Conferences involving 32 families, and has data from 330 evaluation forms from participants (37 of which were from professionals), along with the observation of 28 Conferences and other relevant data.

## The UK research

The research in the UK so far has involved the studies of individual pilot projects, all linked to the Family Partners project reported here. Other studies of individual projects are currently under way, along with a second phase of the Family Partners programme and a new research programme, called 'Pulling Together' which will look particularly at child protection, family culture and longer term outcomes in two new projects.

The studies of individual projects took place in the early periods, and it was clear that practice improved over the time period that was covered (Barker & Barker, 1995). The research covered a full range of child welfare work and involved the following data.

In Hampshire there were 11 families involved in the study, interviews were carried out with the co-ordinators, questionnaires were available from 35 information givers, and interviews were held with 71 of the 101 family members involved (Lupton *et al.*, 1995). Further work is being carried out on both these and subsequent Conferences in Hampshire, together with some comparisons with existing systems. In Wandsworth a small study involved ten interviews with members of four families, and interviews with two mothers of two other families who had declined the offer of a Family Group Conference (Rosen, 1994). In Gwynedd the evaluation focused on Welsh speaking families involved with seven Family Group Conferences, and interviews were carried out with 28 family members, 5 co-ordinators and 12 professionals.

The second phase of the Family Partners programme will be able to continue follow up work on some of the 99 children in the study, and add work in specific areas such as information for families and the development of monitoring and feedback. A report is due in mid-1998. The new programme, Pulling Together, will involve a focus on child protection and the work of a range of agencies, and will include evaluation with around 50 families in the new Wiltshire project and 25 in Haringey, where the work has also involved particular developments for a population with a very wide ranging background of race, language, religion and culture. First reports on this work are due in late 1997, with the work continuing until Easter 1999.

## International research: key themes

We shall see in the forthcoming chapters that the research from around the world broadly reflects that carried out in the UK. To avoid repetition we shall only note below the connection with the UK work when the results from elsewhere show a difference. Such differences as there are broadly reflect the context of either established legislation or the particular focus, for example on abuse and on community. The main themes of the research are outlined below.

### *Membership*

The average number of family members attending the Conferences in both New Zealand and Australia has been around six (Boffa, 1995:

p. 15; Paterson & Harvey, 1991: p. 12). The child or young person is nearly always present in New Zealand, and a substantial minority of Conferences, around one third, have a support person at the Conference (Paterson & Harvey, 1991: pp. 12–15). There is a wide range of attendance, from quite small up to 19 family members. The only contrast with the UK is that in New Zealand there were usually rather more professionals present – around three to four attended – a difference which is not surprising given the much greater number of Family Group Conferences held in New Zealand and their place within the legal system.

The work in Canada was based in three distinct communities in Newfoundland, which have an overall population of around a half a million (Pennell & Burford, 1995b: p. 9). It was developed via strong roots in the relevant communities and focused on the issue of abuse and domestic violence, covering a very wide pattern of abuse and violence within the home, and working hard and successfully to include perpetrators, both male and female, within the Conferences (Pennell & Burford, 1995b: pp. 64–65). Children under 12 did not normally attend the Conferences, and 50 out of 60 people wanted a support person, with young people often picking a relative, guidance counsellor or foster parent for their support (Pennell & Burford, 1995b: p. 88). Besides the person abused it was also often the case that the abuser wanted and needed support, and this appeared valuable in keeping anger under control during the Conferences. Family attendance was high, with an average of over 10 and a range of 4 to 22, and there was usually an average of between two and three professionals present (Pennell & Burford, 1995b: p. 127).

## Process

Preparation for the Conferences in New Zealand and Canada was spread over a number of weeks, with an average in Canada of around $3\frac{1}{2}$ weeks, and rather more in New Zealand (Paterson & Harvey, 1991: p. 20; Pennell & Burford, 1995b: p. 68). The Canadian Conferences, unsurprisingly given the complex abuse situations, took more hours of co-ordinator time to prepare for (around 40 hours: G. Burford, personal communication) and lasted longer, with an average of $5\frac{1}{2}$ hours (Pennell & Burford, 1995b: p. 180). The New Zealand Conferences were more likely to take place in the social services department offices, with around one third being held there, and only a small minority, 16%, were held outside office hours (Paterson & Harvey, 1991: pp. 19–20). Any differences with the UK reflect the different contexts.

Pennell and Burford were able to observe the Conferences, and note that fears that violence would erupt were unfounded. They describe the process of decision-making as predominantly a democratic one (Pennell & Burford, 1995b: p. 160), and note that the return of the co-ordinator and professional(s) at the end of the private family time had some, but not much, influence on the decision-making process.

## Views

In general, as in the UK, practitioners say that they support this approach (Robertson, 1996). Families find it tiring but productive, and different from other social services meetings (Boffa, 1995: pp. 15–17; Swain, 1993: pp. 82–83) in that they seemed less like 'a ratification of professional views' (Ban & Swain, 1994b: p. 13). In the Melbourne study the model was thought to have engaged families who were otherwise hostile to the department (Boffa, 1995: p. 15), a view also echoed by Pennell and Burford (1995b: p. 134). In all the studies Conferences have been successful in gaining a wide range of family attendance (Swain, 1993; Boffa, 1995; Pennell & Burford, 1995b; Robertson, 1996). Family attendees seem quite resilient, for example teenagers in the Newfoundland abuse study generally wanted to attend, saying that they did not want to be 'quarantined out' because of their abuse (Pennell & Burford, 1995b: p. 145). Overall family views may best be summed up by the Canadian finding (Pennell & Burford, 1995b: p. 158), that 90% agreed that it was the right people making the decisions.

### Youth justice

The major New Zealand study on youth justice found poor practice regarding the attendance of victims (some not asked, many asked perfunctorily, few prepared and not much overall attention to their needs). Nonetheless about 60% of victims found attending the Conference to be 'helpful, positive and rewarding' and around 70% of young people and their families expressed satisfaction at the outcomes, even when the decisions were relatively severe (Maxwell & Morris, 1996: p. 100). An Australian study found the great majority of victims being very positive, with 93% expressing satisfaction (T. Goodes, personal communication).

## Outcomes

The great majority of the child welfare Conferences reach agreement between family members and professionals regarding plans to promote the welfare of the child, with Paterson and Harvey (1991: p. 30), in New Zealand, reporting around 92% reaching agreement, and the Mason inquiry (1992) also finding similar percentages. The Newfoundland study found that of the 293 individual participants only 7 stated that they were unhappy with the plan, with 15 not being sure (Pennell & Burford, 1995b: p. 223). These outcomes were mirrored in the Melbourne studies (for example, Lagay *et al.*, 1994: pp. 49–51; Swain, 1993: p. 77) and Boffa (1995: p. 18) reports that the plans were seen by staff as addressing risks to the child and as durable.

Pennell and Burford (1995b: p. 177) comment on the link between private family time and outcomes, as they found that private time was:

> 'essential to promote unification between the generations and sides of the family. Without this, the members are left with the impression that it is the professionals who will look out for the long range interests of the children. As long as the family members acknowledged that there was a problem with family violence or neglect, and that the survivor, if any, was not to blame, they were positioned to come up with sound plans'.

The plans from the Conference still result in a substantial welfare involvement (Robertson, 1996: pp. 59–60), and the services requested seem fairly similar to those via other models of practice, with the Canadian study (Pennell & Burford, 1995b: pp. 228–229) finding a little more emphasis on some material things, for example a washer and dryer, a bed, a video and children's safety devices for stairs and stoves.

### Youth justice

In common with the child welfare Conferences, the great majority of youth justice ones, 95%, reach agreement (Maxwell & Morris, 1996: p. 93). Offence-related factors were found to affect outcome, alongside, just as in the courts, a high proportion of non-offence-related factors. When the recommendations go to a court over 80% are followed, and in general the recommendations involve active penalties. The use of court time and the use of custody has dropped. Only 6% of victims do not want to attend, and there is some evidence that the process has a small effect on recidivism (Maxwell & Morris, 1996: pp. 105–106).

## Co-ordinators

All studies comment on the central role of the co-ordinator, which in youth justice has the additional dimension of dealing with the police and prosecution systems for each Conference. The job is both demanding and difficult. Lagay and his colleagues call for 'attention to the professional development and support of conveners' (Lagay *et al.*, 1994: p. 55), and Boffa (1995) emphasises the need for independence. Paterson and Harvey conclude that 'the success of Family Group Conferences was crucially dependent on Co-ordinators having the appropriate attitudes and skills' (1991: p. 53), a view echoed by Pennell and Burford (1995b) and the Mason (1992) inquiry.

## Conclusions

The overall results from research and development around the world are very positive, and as we shall see they bear great similarities to the outcomes in the UK. However while it is quite clear that the Conferences do generally succeed, implementation problems are evident everywhere, with professional staff finding it difficult to turn their general commitment into specific action to support the model, and with co-ordinators needing to be carefully selected, trained and supported.

It is clear that the Conferences, despite many misgivings regarding the difficult and often warring families that come, have been able to get good attendance and good agreements. They have reached high levels of satisfaction, produced plans that are acceptable to professionals and they have made some impact on a number of problems such as dealing with abusers, helping young people have a voice and providing some *restoration* between victims and offenders. In common with most child welfare practice there are many issues still to resolve, but certainly the international evidence is that the development of Family Group Conferences seems to be involving the right people and making the right decisions in many different areas of child welfare and youth justice.

# Chapter 6

# The Process: Family Group Conferences in Action

In this chapter we move back to the pilot projects to consider how the Family Group Conferences worked in practice. Were they really any different from other meetings people had been to? What were the significant differences? What did people think about the different elements and stages of the meeting? What were the main difficulties encountered? Did people like the process, and would they use it again?

We start by looking at the details of the meetings, both the practicalities and the process, identifying factors that seem different from other child welfare planning meetings. The discussion covers the role of the independent co-ordinator, and who is invited to and attends the Conference. Although comparison is difficult, we consider the contrasts with other child welfare meetings, before looking in some detail at views of difference stages of the Conference process. Finally we consider some of the overall views that the participants have about the Conferences, drawing in part on the evaluation studies undertaken in the project areas by Lupton and her colleagues (1995), Barker and Barker (1995), Rosen (1994), and Thomas (1994), as described in Chapter 5, particularly for information on family views.

## The Conference members

The Conferences appear to have a different membership from other sorts of child welfare meetings. To explore the extent and nature of this difference we shall look in turn at the co-ordinator, the family members and the professionals.

### The co-ordinator

Managing the practicalities and the process of the meeting is the responsibility of the co-ordinator, a new role which clearly differentiates the Family Group Conference from other meetings. But how much does this role really change the nature of the meeting?

*Difference and independence*

Family members, who are probably not well versed in the intricacies of
the different jobs within social services, seem surprisingly able to
appreciate that the co-ordinator's role is different from that of social
workers in general. Barker and Barker (1995) found that family
members, particularly those attending the later conferences, could
clearly describe the different roles undertaken by the co-ordinator and
the key worker. The majority of their respondents were clear that the
co-ordinator was independent of social services.

Rosen (1994) reports all family members being very appreciative of
the skills of the co-ordinator, particularly in explaining the process and
the concerns about the child clearly and understandably. The preparation work with family members was thought to be crucial:

> 'A lot of work was done with the co-ordinator before the meeting.
> This was very important as you need to know what you are going to
> focus on. In a tense situation you can so easily blank out.'

> (family member quoted by Rosen)

The Winchester study similarly reported that 'although a few family
members failed to differentiate the co-ordinators from any other professionals, the majority did appear to appreciate the independence of
their role' (Lupton *et al.*, 1995: p. 107). They also report that the co-
ordinators themselves valued their independence highly, seeing it as
essential to the establishment of family, as opposed to professional,
ownership of the Conference process.

Our interviews with co-ordinators have given a similar picture: that
their independence from the provision of services and case management
is vital to the process. As one co-ordinator put it, the family has: 'got to
feel that you are impartial ... they need to see you've got their interests
at heart, what they say to you is confidential and you're not going to go
and share it with the social worker'. The independence would seem to
be primarily focused on role and not on location or employer, as there
were different employment practices in different projects in the study.

The co-ordinators maintain their independence by striving not to be
drawn into too much detail of the past, from either the family or the
professional point of view. They try to maintain impartiality, perhaps
by being sensitive to the fact that the social worker's agenda, as one co-
ordinator put it, may not be 'the same as the family's agenda. As the co-
ordinator I was not prepared to take on board the social worker's
agenda only. That was not my prime concern, my prime concern was to
make sure that the family had all the information they required in order
to help them deal with the thing'.

All the evidence we have is that the independent role of the co-
ordinator creates the conditions for the wider family, despite their
differences, to meet at the Family Group Conference and sort out

problems in their own way. Interesting and worthwhile meetings may be able to take place without the co-ordinator role, but these are likely to be more susceptible to being overtaken by the professionals' agenda. In Hereford, where the absence of independent co-ordinators meant that the social worker did a lot of the setting up of the meeting in discussion with a more independent *chair*, the meetings were sometimes convened to ratify or explain decisions already taken by the social services. The family's agenda did not appear to be as fully explored, and there was scope for greater emphasis on the social services' decision being for the best. Whereas most of the social workers we spoke to were positive about the need for independence in the role of the co-ordinator, a third of those from Hereford did not see the role as different, several of them confusing it with the child protection co-ordinator, who chairs child protection conferences.

Many social workers described the benefits of the co-ordinator being neutral, less threatening, facilitative and arbitrating from both points of view. They suggested this made them more acceptable to families suspicious of social workers. Interestingly, several social workers said that the independent role was important for the professionals as well:

> 'It's very meaningful for the agency to have the unusual experience of being invited to family meetings by an independent co-ordinator. It certainly causes some problems at the outset because people were saying "well, who are these co-ordinators ... they're taking over our cases and what does it mean". So I think that maybe even more for the agencies than the families it's significant that they are independent and they don't get sucked into the issues that we might get drawn into.'

### Time taken for setting up the meeting

Once allocated to the role, the co-ordinator spent an average of 22 hours setting up the meeting. Sometimes the job was easy and could be done in 10 hours or so, at other times 30 or more hours work was needed. These hours were spread out over different time periods, with the majority taking between 2 and 4 weeks, but the range being from 1 to 20 weeks. The length of time taken was affected by many different, mainly 'family' factors. For instance in one case the family went 'on holiday' to their country of origin for some weeks; in another arrangements to have a father escorted from prison to the Conference took time to put in place. Often it was difficult to arrange a time and date mutually satisfactory to all the main participants, and sometimes the co-ordinator was fitting the work in alongside another job. In a few cases, the time from referral to meeting caused problems because the social workers involved felt *in limbo* and unsure of how to continue work with the family. It needed to be clearer to these workers that the model does not preclude on-going work with the family, and that there is no question of the social workers handing over responsibility for the case to the co-ordinators. The clarification of the co-ordinator's role and his or her relationship with the social worker would seem to be vital to the smooth running of the process.

## Which family members are invited?

One of the aims of the model is to involve the wider family in the process. How successful were the projects, once having identified the family group, in inviting and assembling family members?

Amongst the identified family, the *potential invitees*, there were quite often one or two, and occasionally a whole group, whom the child or parent(s) did not want to invite. Sometimes the co-ordinator could persuade them to set aside their apparent prejudices and invite these family members, but in over a third of Conferences some remained excluded. The unwanted relative was most often a close male relative of the young person or mother. Sometimes there was no clear reason for the wish to exclude individuals or groups other than 'I don't want them poking their nose into our affairs' or to 'protect' elderly relatives from shock or upset, or pressure to help (Barker & Barker, 1995: p. 5); sometimes it was explicit that the reason for excluding the relative was past abuse. Once invitations had been negotiated with the family, the co-ordinators did not feel it necessary to exclude anyone else themselves.

Exclusions aside, the size and membership of the family group invited to the Conference varied greatly, with an average of seven, but a range from one Conference with only three invited, through to one Conference with 20 invited family members. Invitees included parents, step-parents and cohabitees, ex-step-parents and ex-cohabitees, grandparents, step-grandparents, aunts, uncles, siblings, half-siblings, step-siblings, siblings' partners and ex-partners, cousins, great aunts, parents' friends, neighbours, peers and peers' parents. In other words, the family group represented the whole range of possible family structures and cultures from the close knit to the loose knit, and from kin to friends.

### Family views of family group invitations

Family members were on the whole positive about the composition of the family group, with 84% saying that the right family members had been invited (Lupton *et al.*, 1995: p. 88). Barker and Barker reported that any regrets participants had after the Conference were about their decisions *not* to invite people. Relatives are often pleased to be invited, as this gives them *permission* to become involved in a situation that has been causing anxiety, but there are sometimes mixed feelings about the participation of *friends*, which seems to be related to the power or influence their attendance bestows upon them.

## Which family members attend?

Bearing in mind that 68% of the families were separated or divorced, it is some evidence of family members' courage and commitment, as well as co-ordinators' skills, that the great majority of those invited went on to attend. Conferences had an average of six family members attending, with a range of two to eleven.

In respect of family attendance, therefore, the Conferences are very different from other planning meetings. For example Thoburn and her colleagues (1995: p. 129) reported that 31% of 'very important' supporting family members were *not* invited to child protection conferences in her study, and that overall 22 relatives and 13 friends attended 220 conferences. The Family Group Conferences were dramatically different, with the 80 Conferences in the study attended by 337 relatives and friends alongside a total of 127 parent figures. It is interesting to note, in the context of debates about who is family, that in over a quarter a friend or neighbour was present, and in 15% the young person had a peer supporter attending.

### Parent attendance

We looked particularly at the pattern of invitation and attendance of parents at the Family Group Conferences. Parents were represented at 96% of the possible Conferences. Of the other Conferences, some concerned children bereaved of both parents and in one case a young person did not want to invite her surviving parent. In four instances no parent was present when they could have been. Both natural parents attended over half of the meetings, despite the rate of separation or divorce, and a step-parent or cohabitee attended a quarter of the meetings. Male parent figures were more likely to decline the invitation as compared to female parent figures (22% compared to 9%), but this remains a fairly low percentage (see Table 6.1). These findings are very different from Thoburn's relating to family attendance at the child protection conferences (Table 6.2).

It should be noted that Thoburn's study was undertaken some years before the Family Group Conference research, and local authorities could be expected to have expended more effort on involving parents in the child protection process since then.

Comparison can also be made with other sorts of child welfare planning meetings which involve both family and professionals. For example, with data gathered much more recently on parent and child attendance at the review meetings held for children in the care system

**Table 6.1** Parents and parent figures invited and attending Family Group Conferences.

| Invited and attended | % | Invited, did not attend | % |
|---|---|---|---|
| Mother and father alone | 42 | Mother | 8 |
| Single parent | 28 | Father | 14 |
| Mother, father and partner(s) | 13 | Stepmother | 1 |
| One parent and partner | 10 | Stepfather | 8 |
| Step-parent alone | 3 | | |

**Table 6.2** Comparison of carers'/parents' and non-resident parents' attendance at Family Group Conferences and at child protection conferences.

| | At FGC (%) | CPC (%) |
|---|---|---|
| Main carer/parent attended | 93 all | 36 all or part |
| Non-resident parent attended | 48 | 30 all or part |

(Grimshaw, 1996). This research also highlights the different membership of the Family Group Conference (Table 6.3).

### Children's attendance

The Family Group Conference process is certainly successful in involving adults, but how does it succeed with children and young people? Young people were expected to attend the Family Group Conference in almost all instances, and were free to be present for as much of the meeting as they wanted. Of those over the age of 10 who were invited all attended except four who refused to attend. Sometimes the social worker or the carer(s) decided the child(ren) should not be asked to attend. This was more likely to happen where their ages were between 5 and 12, and in these cases the co-ordinators debated the issue, but in the end accepted the carer's decision.

Attendance of the children who were the subject of the meeting

**Table 6.3** Comparison of parents' attendance at Family Group Conferences and at Review meetings.

| | At FGC (%) | At Reviews (%) |
|---|---|---|
| Mother | 85 | 44 |
| Father | 61 | 21 |

compares favourably with those found to attend child protection conferences (Thoburn et al., 1995), and at both the review meetings and the planning meetings held for children in the care system (Grimshaw, 1996) (Table 6.4).

**Table 6.4** Comparison of children's and young persons' attendance at Family Group Conferences and at Review meetings, planning meetings and child protection conferences.

| | At FGC (%) | At reviews (%) | At planning meetings (%) | At CPC (%) |
|---|---|---|---|---|
| Child <5 | 45 | 9 | 10 | — |
| Child 5–10 | 39 | 30 | 11 | — |
| Child 11–15 | 90 | 80 | 46 | } 11 to all, |
| Child 16–18 | 66 | 55 | 75 | } or part |

Professionals we spoke to often worried that the young people would not be able to cope with attending a Family Group Conference. Social workers sometimes wanted to protect their young clients from conflict or rejection and preferred them not to attend a meeting which might present such views. Co-ordinators, on the other hand, felt that it was important for young people to hear what was being said, and to make their own views known. They saw their role as helping to ensure the young person had an advocate, and that all the participants were prepared to focus on the child's needs. They would only consider excluding a child if it was anticipated that they would be scapegoated by all the other participants. The other professionals we spoke to all thought that the young person should have the opportunity to be there, but opinions differed on how far they should be encouraged to attend, and how able they were to cope with any ensuing unpleasantness. The majority were of the opinion that their attendance was, as one put it, painful but appropriate.

Of the young people who were the subject of the meeting, eleven were interviewed in local evaluation studies (seven in one project, four in another) representing a quarter of those 10 years and above. Although this is a fairly small sample and their views cover a wide range, the young people are generally positive. They felt they should be asked and should take part, although they had been nervous and sometimes uncomfortable in the meeting (Lupton et al., 1995: pp. 96–100). In the one Conference where the process was abandoned because of family upset, professionals had been very concerned about the effect of the meeting on the young girl. However the research found that she and the family could take the view that 'at least they knew where they stood' and were therefore in a position to make future decisions based on the reality of the situation (Barker and Barker, 1995: p. 9). They too seemed to take the view that her attendance was 'painful but appropriate'.

## Which professionals attend?

In the Family Group Conference model, only those professionals with direct and relevant information about a child are invited to attend. The co-ordinator discussed with the child and carers which professionals should be there; on average two professionals attended. This means that the ratio of professionals to family is on average two to six. The number of professionals in the Conferences studied ranged up to five, but in only two of the 80 Conferences were the family outnumbered by professionals.

This is in marked contrast to many other decision-making processes in child welfare, where the one or two family members invited are outnumbered. For instance, the great majority of child protection conferences studied by Thoburn had six or more professionals attending, with almost a fifth having more than ten. An earlier study (Shemmings & Thoburn, 1990: p. 20) noted that, of the professionals present, 63% had met the parents, but only 51% had met the child, and 21% had met neither. Where there are large numbers of professionals attending, many are likely to be unknown to the family, increasing family dissatisfaction with the process (McGloin & Turnbull, 1986: pp. 46–48). It is in some contrast that 87% of family members said that the right professionals had been present at the Family Group Conference (Lupton *et al.*, 1995: p. 88).

Most often, the professionals attending were from the social services, usually the case worker together with their team leader, or a resource team member, or a residential care worker. Where other professionals were invited, they were most often teachers or other representatives from education. Other invitees included health visitors, doctors or psychiatrists, probation officers, police, home care workers, guardians *ad litem*. Those invited did not always attend; teachers were the most likely to respond positively to the invitation, doctors were the least likely. Co-ordinators recognised that attendance might not be easy:

'You do feel slightly embarrassed asking other professionals. If you're wanting others for instance you've got school teachers there who have come very much out of hours that they work, or child guidance or drugs advisor. You have a feeling that if they're committed they'll come and if they're not committed they'll probably find an excuse anyway.'

The attendance or non-attendance of other professionals as *information givers* did on occasion cause difficulties. The projects remained very localised, and despite attempts to get multi-agency involvement in the implementation process, many of the professionals invited to the meetings were not aware of the model or its implications for their contribution. Co-ordinators might spend hours trying to contact professionals, sending literature, explaining the Conference process to them and helping them to clarify their contribution to the meeting. Sometimes this led to very useful information, and support, for family members attending:

> '[The prison] were marvellous, once they knew what was going on they were very sympathetic. The probation officer was quite inconvenienced by it all and could have been very difficult with me, but he was great, he was very good.'

On other occasions problems engaging other professionals in the process could lead to difficulties. For example, non-attendance of important information givers:

> 'Because the health visitor wasn't there, the social worker ended up having to justify the medical stuff. Well, it's just not on.'

> 'It took me I don't know how many phone calls to get the faintest response from the psychiatrist and she didn't come and she sent a very unhelpful report.'

Some of the information givers themselves complained that they had had short notice of the meeting and that it was a bit much to expect attendance out of working hours. They were often sceptical about the meeting beforehand, but almost always thought afterwards that it had been useful. Some had felt inadequately prepared, but the majority were pleased to have attended.

## The practicalities of the Conferences

The practical details of the Conferences were handled by the co-ordinators, from the provision of information leaflets, through to the booking of a room, and the arranging of refreshments.

### Leaflets

Some co-ordinators made reference to sending out leaflets to families before they first met, but the majority did not mention this and it is not known how often family members received written information about the model. Barker and Barker's study (1995) found that few family members had read the leaflet, or could even remember receiving one, although they could sometimes locate it in a pile of papers when asked. It would seem that written information is felt to be important by social services but is not, in fact, seen to be very useful by family members, at least in the form available. The leaflets were, of course, a source of information for other professionals as well, and may have been better received by them, but we have not explored this.

### Time of day

While it is very rare for professionals to arrange case meetings outside working hours, in Family Group Conferences the family is involved in deciding the time of day, and evenings or weekends are positive options. A third of the Conferences were held outside working hours. Sometimes co-ordinators steered the family towards a time that suited themselves, and often they advised families to take account of the potential length of the meeting, so that enough time was allowed. The time of day was therefore usually negotiated between the family members and the co-ordinator. Time of day is likely to affect the attendance rate of professionals.

### Venue

The family is encouraged to choose a venue for the meeting that is convenient to the majority of the attendees, but on *neutral territory* so that all participants can feel more at ease. The most popular sites were family centres, but leisure centres, village halls, community centres, voluntary organisation offices and hotels were all used. Only four of the 80 meetings were not held on neutral territory; two were held in social service department offices and two in the family's home. The choice of neutral territory was thought to have a significant influence on the meeting by family members and professionals alike.

It was important that the venue provided suitable accommodation. The ideal venue would seem to be one that has three rooms (one for the family, one for the co-ordinator and others to wait in, and one for children or others to withdraw to), a kitchen for refreshments and outdoor space for children, smokers or others to escape to for a while.

Co-ordinators put much effort into finding suitable venues; often when they had found appropriate premises, they might suggest it to the next family, and also alert other co-ordinators in the project to it. In this way, the projects could develop a list of available and suitable venues across the project area. In North Wales, where there were no family centres and co-ordinators had the additional problem of working with families in isolated villages, hotels were generally found to be very suitable for meetings. While on one occasion the cost of a rather 'posh' hotel was queried by management, from the co-ordinator and family point of view it was very comfortable, and the surroundings helped to defuse much of the tension.

*Refreshments*

All the co-ordinators made sure there was tea and coffee available, with biscuits, and often sandwiches. They learnt that it was important to provide crisps and fizzy drinks for the children, and a smoking area for desperate adults. In one project the co-ordinators routinely arranged for a meal to be prepared or brought in for the family, who could state their preferences beforehand. This was thought to give the family a clear practical signal that the Conference might need a long time, as well as being a sign of valuing the family.

*Meeting length*

In the Family Group Conference the family is given 'as long as it takes' to make a plan. This means that the length of the meeting cannot be predicted: there is no planned finishing time. We found the average Conference to be just over $2\frac{1}{2}$ hours, but with a wide range of 1 to 6 hours. Of this, about half is usually spent by the family alone. There was a significant difference in the length of the meeting between projects: where a meal was offered, the meetings were longer.

The inability of the co-ordinator to predict how long the meeting will be can cause difficulties for those attending and affect the choice of time and venue for the meeting. We heard a few instances of meetings being a little rushed because of family members having to leave, and because other people were waiting to use the room. Some information givers, other than the social worker, leave after the first part of the meeting, and so do not hear about the family's plan or the part they might be being asked to play in it. This could cause problems, but it would be difficult for most professionals to set aside the somewhat unknown time, which could be up to six hours, for one meeting. Of course contact could be made by telephone, and one key professional, the social worker, is very likely to stay throughout, and will certainly be involved in the discussions of the plan at the Conference.

If information givers must leave then it is important for the family that the resources they could call on are clearly defined in the first stage, enabling them to make realistic plans. If information givers are not present when the plan is discussed then it is important for them that prompt feedback is given regarding the meeting's outcome. Where this had not happened, information givers, quite rightly, complained.

## The process

Views on process and outcome are likely to be interlinked. We will focus in this chapter on what we have learnt about the process, stage by stage, before we consider the outcomes of the Conferences in Chapter

8. As we shall see the *process* is, in the eyes of the participants, a very important part of experience.

## Setting the meeting up

Before the Conference itself there is the process of setting it up, which is the bulk of the co-ordinator's work. Many of the people we spoke to acknowledged the importance of this preparation for the success of the meeting. The Family Group Conference cannot be considered simply as a meeting but as a process from referral to distribution of an agreed plan. The 'setting up the meeting' includes contacting family members, identifying who is family, inviting and persuading family members and other professionals to attend, helping family to focus on the task at hand, agreeing a venue, date and time, and facilitating attendance at the meeting. The detailed management of this process, and of the three stages of the meeting, is considered in the next chapter.

## The information giving stage

The first stage of the Conference, and even the *settling in* time before it starts, sets both the tone and the agenda for the meeting. The prime difference from other meetings is that the information is provided for the family at the family's meeting. The professionals give information on the concerns for the family discussion, including information on the parameters of acceptability and their statutory duties, and also on the range of possible resources available to enable successful solutions to be found. Information needs to be clear, and opinions need to be substantiated, which demands a new art of report writing.

Information givers were generally clear that their role was to provide information on the concerns being expressed, but it was sometimes less clear to them that they were also there to provide information on the services or resources they could offer to the family (Lupton *et al.*, 1995: p. 79).

Social workers, particularly those more experienced in using Family Group Conferences, were articulate about the difficulties in presenting sensitive information to families. The full and wordy reports they were used to presenting to child protection conferences were not appropriate, and so they had to learn new ways of communicating. This new way of working was at first challenging and often frightening to the social workers, not least because the family were able to ask questions about the information.

> 'I felt more nervous about presenting information in a useful and accessible way. I would say this is a positive feature – if uncomfortable for me.'

> (social worker, in Lupton *et al.*, 1995: p. 80)

Both co-ordinators and social workers commented on how the practice of giving information to the families had changed with experience:

> 'Then the social worker introduced the problems and she did it very well, she was very clear, which was in marked contrast to meetings she had done previously, she had really improved and learnt how to manage the meeting.'

> (co-ordinator)

> 'My practice has changed a lot since then, I do things differently. I cringe now about how I did, or rather I didn't, present information to the family.'

> (social worker)

Often attempts were made by the professionals to present information in such a way as to give the young person's perspective. Sometimes this was found to be very influential, but of course presenting the information does not guarantee that the family will take notice of it: one co-ordinator described a frustrating instance of the family ignoring or belittling an information giver who was putting the child's view. However, it was clear that the right information given in the right way could have a great impact on the family members:

> 'So we started off with people talking about the children and that was very very powerful. The nursery worker was presenting that [the boy] had become very very unhappy, very disturbed, quite aggressive to other children, very different over the last three months or so.'

### Family views of the information giving

The great majority of family members thought that the information giving session had been handled well. Although a small number had felt uncomfortable (17%) they thought they had had an opportunity to speak (86%) and had felt able to ask questions (80%). There was some criticism of reports being too long, too focused on the negatives, and too full of jargon, particularly in the earlier meetings. There was also the feeling early on amongst family members that they would have liked more information to help them plan for the child (Lupton *et al.*, 1995: p. 87).

Barker and Barker found that family members appreciated the social workers' presentation of facts from the young person's perspective, as this could change their view of the situation and alert them to possible solutions (1995: p. 9). They also found that most family members appreciated receiving written material, 'as they felt it provided a clear structure for all stages of the meeting. Less assertive members found it useful as a tool with which to remind others that there was an agenda to address. These members felt this prevented the hijacking of the meeting by *powerful* or more articulate people and also served to prioritise the rights and welfare of the child/young person' (Barker and Barker, 1995: p. 8).

## The issue of confidentiality

Professionals we spoke to often voiced concerns about disclosing confidential information to the wider family group. Clearly there are concerns about who has the right to know personal information, and about the way that the information will subsequently be kept confidential or not. These questions are not unique to Family Group Conferences. At a child protection conference, for example, there are similar issues about permission to disclose information, and about what may happen to that information afterwards. In accord with the best practice there, co-ordinators tried to ensure that there would be no surprises about the information relayed at the start of the Conference, and they were careful to emphasise at the Conference that information was only being given in the interests of the child or children, that it should be solely related to the concerns about their welfare and should be regarded as confidential by those present.

As in child protection conferences the ideal of 'nothing should be a surprise when they get to the meeting' may not always be reached. A minority of family members are not always prepared for what is to be shared at the meeting. Lupton reports 21% of adult family members complaining about the confidential or personal details that were provided during the information-giving session. In addition, two of the nine young people interviewed said they had been embarrassed by the information presented. It would, of course, be surprising if there was not some discomfort with the discussion of personal problems. In contrast, the other studies did not raise confidentiality as a particular issue for family members. There is some evidence that practice improved as co-ordinators and professionals became more skilled at the process, for example Barker and Barker (1995) found that social workers learnt how to present relevant information clearly, and to omit information not relevant to the concerns: this reduced criticisms of this stage of the meeting. It appears that the professionals' concerns about confidentiality at Family Group Conferences was not generally shared by family members.

## The private family time

In almost all cases, the family were left alone during the meeting, to discuss the information and formulate a plan. In three of the projects the private family time was completely mandatory, there was no debate about it, and suitable ways were found to prepare families for this both beforehand and at the Conference.

The fourth project, in Hereford and Worcester, did not press ahead so strongly with the private family time but *offered* it to the family. Because of this, five of the eleven families had a professional with them while they debated the information given. Although the professionals involved report that they did not participate much, we can only speculate on the effect their presence had on the family, and on the difference between private family time and non-private family time. Apart from these five families in the one area, only one other asked the co-ordinator to stay, and this was for a second Conference.

Seventy-four Family Group Conferences therefore had private family time. We do not know exactly what went on in any of these discussions, although we do know that there were no incidents of violence. That is not to say that the family members found it an easy task, nor to say that there were no disagreements, but that families did manage to meet and discuss. As we noted before, this in itself was quite a surprise to some social workers.

### What did the professionals feel about leaving the families?

In our interviews with social workers, some of whom had attended Conferences and some not, the predominant opinion was that the private family time was a very important element of the Conference model, and might even be crucial to it working at its best. Those who had tried the model were the most enthusiastic but almost all of them appreciated that there were advantages. As one social worker said:

'That's how it is anyway because even if I go along, like, every day of the week, the family still have the majority of the time with themselves and will make decisions amongst themselves anyway. So, I mean I think that's the way it is, that's the most effective vehicle for change.'

The enthusiasm for the private family time in theory did not necessarily make it easy for social workers to accept it in practice:

'There are fears about what if they are colluding or arranging things behind our back.'

'That would be the hardest thing for me to adjust to. It's quite hard for social workers – wanting to know exactly everything that's been said and I think we're used to being partly involved in every aspect of things. But I do think that's important for the family's sake because they always know each other better than we do and they know lots of things about each other that we don't know and maybe don't need to know.'

Others took a sanguine view:

'If the family wants to have a slanging match amongst themselves, let them get on with it and there is no reason why social workers or professionals should be involved. As long as at the end of it they come up with a workable plan, how they get to it is their business.'

'Of course a lot of that is already going on. The co-ordinator goes out to talk to the family preparing them for the Family Group Conference and immediately they start getting on the phone to each other and talking in smaller groups and doing preparatory work. Sometimes they just come to the meeting to present a plan they have already cooked up, if you like.'

The *local* research studies similarly found overall support for the family private time from information givers, with attendant anxieties that particular families would not manage to use it productively, and curiosity as to what was being discussed. All the staff interviewed by Barker and Barker (1995) spoke of 'unfounded fears' about the family meeting together. They worried that rows would break out or that the child would be scapegoated or that the social worker would be blamed. At the meeting, they found that hearing raised voices from the family made them anxious, and they were uncertain how to respond. However their experience of the meeting was that there were rows but this did not prohibit the family from making a plan, or prevent participants supporting vulnerable members.

Only one of the Conferences in the study appeared to involve some family time that was not being used profitably to discuss the child's needs. There was no doubt in the others that the family used the private time to discuss the information presented, and to formulate a plan. That is not to say that that is all that was discussed. Some social workers found it hard to come to terms with the fact that there might be some bursts of laughter, with a little bit of the meeting actually appearing enjoyable; an unexpected but positive aspect of the Conference.

### Did the families think having private time was a good idea?

If professionals were anxious about leaving families alone, what did the families themselves feel? Both the Rosen (1994) and the Barker and Barker (1995) studies found that family members were also sometimes anxious about being left on their own, fearing that their family lacked the practical or emotional resources to participate. They were appreciative of the co-ordinator's work in preparing them for their role in the meeting and the overall feeling of the family members was that it had not been as difficult as anticipated.

Lupton and her colleagues (1995: p. 88) found that the great majority of family members (89%) thought it was easier or as easy to talk as a family group without the professionals being present. Only 11% thought it more difficult to talk without professionals. A minority (27%) said that some problems had developed during the family discussion because the professionals were not there. Some of these referred to needing more information and to seeking out professionals to provide this; others felt that the family had not been able to lead or control the meeting as much as they would have liked. A few family members felt quite strongly that the professionals should have remained. However, there were equally positive comments from family members about being left alone:

'I don't think we'd have come up with so much if the professionals had stayed.'

'I thought professionals would be there when the decision was made, but in the long run it's better because people can express themselves and are not scrutinised by professionals.'

## Debating the plan

When the family felt they had reached agreement, they asked the co-ordinator to come back into the Conference to hear the plan. If information givers were still on the premises, they would also be asked back in; often the social worker would have waited but other professionals would have left. This stage of the meeting was said by co-ordinators to be the most difficult to manage, and by family members to be the part they remembered least about, because the family was relieved to have accomplished a plan and was exhausted and wanting to go home. The process of recording and clarifying the plan with the family therefore needed to be very efficient, and in practice it sometimes did not receive the time needed.

Although, as we shall see in Chapter 8, most people were happy about the plans made, some were anxious:

'As a manager there have been times when I have panicked about the decisions that've been made at Family Group Conferences. I've thought I wish we'd never let them have that bloody Conference, what have we done, should we have been more directive, you know. Losing a bit of control over the decisions that are made about children's lives. And although people have managed to shut me up, I think it's a learning thing, again for other people taking on Family Group Conferences it's something worth knowing about. Because they're going to have to face the fact that fairly quickly you lose control over things that you've taken for granted that you'll have control over.'

### Monitoring

It is the co-ordinator's responsibility to make sure that the plan is genuinely agreed by all parties, and to make sure that some monitoring is in place. However the form of that monitoring may vary widely from case to case. In most of the cases we looked at (67 of the 80) the social service department was to undertake the monitoring role. In three of these cases the family also had a monitoring role, and in another three agencies such as school and health visitors were involved. In only one case was the responsibility of monitoring placed entirely with the family. One other family did not want any further review or monitoring, which was acceptable to the participants. This means that in 14% of plans, monitoring arrangements were not specified.

Review Conferences were arranged at six of the initial Conferences, and another six arranged a review Conference at a later date. Some reviews were used to continue negotiations for a long-term plan, while others were called because the original plans needed reviewing or revising. Attendance tended to be poorer at review Conferences, but familiarity with the process reduced anxieties about it.

In the Family Group Conference the co-ordinator generally has no further role after the plan has been agreed, written up and circulated. However many expressed personal dissatisfaction with this cut off, while recognising that it has advantages:

> 'Personally I destroy any records I have because I don't feel I should have them. But I want to know what happened and I find that really frustrating not always knowing what happened next. I always have to phone the social worker after a few months and say "what happened?", just for my own personal curiosity really, my need to know.'

> 'I think one of the advantages both for the family and to the co-ordinator is that the "beginning to end" part of the process is clear and distinct and there's no expectation that you are intervening in their lives. Even if your only role left is monitoring, there's still a sense it seems to me of just keeping a little bit of a hold on things. Now maybe there's a need to do that but it feels a little bit like not quite letting go.'

User views on the co-ordinator role *cut off point* are not generally known but some families would like to be able to report on their successes to the co-ordinator:

> 'Actually the feedback from families I've had is that they would like, when the plan is going well, someone to come round and tell them how well it was going, which I hadn't thought about actually.'

We will return to the issue of feedback in Chapter 9.

## The Family Group Conferences that did not happen

Sometimes the co-ordinator cannot manage to get the family to have a Conference as intended. We have looked at the 'Conferences that did not happen' to find out why this occurred and what it can tell us about the process.

It was clear that where referral to the project was supposed to be automatic, rather than being an option for social workers, there were many more failed attempts at convening a Family Group Conference. Effectively there were 18 such failures when the referral was automatic (almost half of all referrals), compared to five in each of the two other projects where it was not automatic (representing 23% and 13% of referrals to those projects). Alongside the 18 there were two thought to be unsuitable because of the nature of the case, and five which were unnecessary because plans had already been made. A further two were thought to be affected by social workers' lack of commitment to the project.

However, of the 18 cases that did not reach a Conference, fully half were resolved by the family before the Conference could be convened. The other half could not be convened because the family refused to cooperate, or withdrew from the process. In the other two projects, similarly, the reason the Conference did not take place was as often because families had resolved their difficulties as because they were refusing to use the process.

We have no way of knowing whether, or how far, the introduction of the model to the family, via the independent co-ordinator, contributed to the resolution, but it seems reasonable to assume that at least some of them were helped by the several contacts made by the co-ordinator. Some examples of each type of 'Conference that did not happen' is given below.

Unsuitable
Following an acrimonious matrimonial separation, two teenage girls were living with their mother. The relationship between the younger of the two, a 13 year old, and the mother was breaking down and a trial of living with the father had been unsuccessful. The co-ordinator found that the girl was being pressurised by the mother and unable to state who she wanted to attend the Conference. Mother only wanted a 16 year old young man, a friend of the family, to attend, and he was felt to be inappropriate as the sole *family* member. The case was agreed to be unsuitable because of the size of the family group. Shortly afterwards the mother declared her relationship with the 16 year old, causing much upset to her daughters, both of whom moved out – the older one to friends, the younger into foster care.

Unclear
A 12 year old girl and her family were automatically referred to the project following registration at the initial child protection conference. The co-ordinator visited the family and made numerous telephone calls. The parents felt that the agreed protection plan had reduced the

problems and worried that a family meeting would disrupt the progress made. The project 'manager' commented that this case was early on in the project, when the referral procedures were still unclear. The Family Group Conference was erroneously being seen as part of the child protection plan, an addition to decisions made, rather than as part of the process. 'If we weren't clear, how could we expect the parents to be?'

Social worker influence

A 13 year old *looked after* boy was automatically referred to the project to discuss the long term plans for his placement. The co-ordinator met with the child twice and then, as there had been various changes, with the social worker and team leader to clarify the situation. Social services were against continuing. The co-ordinator commented

'I believe the social services were concerned about the setting up of a Family Group Conference – they did not see its value for this child because of their knowledge of previous family breakdown/family dynamics etc. The issue is, once the referral has been passed on to you how much do you carry on despite obvious reluctance by the refer-ring agency? I feel the co-ordinator should take their lead from the child and family members themselves not the social services as happened in this case'.

Refusal

A 14 year old girl was being looked after by the local authority after having serious relationship difficulties with her mother. The parents had separated the year before, and the girl had made allegations of sexual abuse against her father. These might have been manipulative, but she did not retract, and so she could not go and stay there any more, although he was the only one who seemed prepared to have her. The mother was engrossed in her new life with a much younger cohabitee, and was very difficult to find in. The venue and date of the meeting had been arranged, family were coming from quite a way away, and an advocate for the girl had been organised. Then the mother said she did not see the point of her sisters coming, and later she rang up to cancel the whole thing because she was going on holiday. The co-ordinator commented that the social worker had had a frustrating time with the family in the previous year, and this was a 'last ditch attempt' which was worth a try. It raised the question in the co-ordinator's mind of whether it would have been worth while to go ahead without the mother.

Refusal

Two boys aged 10 and 12 were being looked after but their placement was breaking down – the referral was to make long-term plans. The parents were separated and both refused point blank to entertain any idea of having the family meet – there was a long-term history of disputes between them. The co-ordinator commented that more time could have been spent on working with the mother but it was not likely that her resistance to the father would have lessened. The boys remained in local authority care.

### Resolution

A 7 year old girl was accommodated at the request of the parent; she had been looked after for a couple of weeks by the time of the referral. The social worker and co-ordinator met with the mother to discuss the Family Group Conference, the needs of the child and what kind of plans the social services department could or could not support. This began to change things radically and the mother started talking about going into a family resource centre with the child, which is what happened. It was subsequently thought that it would have been better to have had a Conference, as the decision might have been experienced differently by the family, and better supported by family members.

### Resolution

A 15 year old boy was placed in a residential unit at the request of his mother, due to his pattern of offending behaviour. The co-ordinator visited the young person, the mother and the father (the parents were separated). Between them they resolved the issue, and the boy returned to live with his father in a nearby village. This arrangement persisted.

The group of 'Family Group Conferences that did not happen' are very varied but do have the following characteristics:

- 50% of cases, where the reason for referral is clear, are resolved between the co-ordinator's first contact with the family and before the convening of the meeting, presumably in part because of the co-ordinator's work.
- If the problem is resolved without a meeting, there is some concern that the plan will have less widespread family support, and will lack necessary detail.

Both of the above points seem to apply across most types of problem and case. How much contribution the co-ordinator makes to the resolution is not clear, and the level of family support for the plan is not known, however a number of themes are worth further examination as our knowledge about the Conferences develops.

Where reason for referral is unclear the co-ordinator's first task will be to clarify the issues to be discussed and planned for. How often do co-ordinators find themselves undertaking a supervisory role with agencies to help them clarify their objectives? What is the likelihood in these cases that the referral will turn out to have been inappropriate or unnecessary?

The co-ordinator has to balance the importance of the different factions in *warring* families. Is it worth continuing without some significant players? How far and for how long should co-ordinators go on trying to engage family members? There is some evidence that where the process is protracted to try to include the sceptical, additional problems can develop leading to withdrawal. On the other hand, some Conferences benefit from co-ordinators who are prepared to go 'that bit further' and are reluctant to give up: cutting corners or 'giving up' early can be detrimental. We do now know what the optimum effort is, but there is some evidence from these and other projects that such factors could contribute to the failure of the process to result in a Conference.

Aside from these issues, the overall message from these findings is quite encouraging: even when the Conference itself does not occur there is a good chance, with a skilled co-ordinator and a reasonably clear referral, that the process of preparing for it will in itself prove of value to the family.

## Participants' views of the model

We have looked at the practical realities of the Family Group Conference process and the participants' views of these. We were also interested in what participants and potential participants think of the model in general. Was it a good idea? Should it be available more widely? Would they use it again?

### Social workers

We asked social workers a number of questions relating to their perceptions of the Family Group Conference: was it different from other meetings, was it empowering for families, would they like the Conference project to continue? Answers to these have been sketched out before (see for example Tables 4.5 and 4.6 in Chapter 4), but they merit further discussion here.

The great majority (92%) said that they thought the model was different from child protection conferences or review meetings. Most saw the difference in terms of the principles behind the meeting: it was the family's meeting rather than the professionals'; roles and power relationships were changed; the family were being asked to take responsibility for making decisions. Some focused more on the process of the meeting itself rather than spelling out the underlying principles: it was less formal, more relaxed; it was not so dominated by professionals or organised according to the professionals' agendas; information was shared differently; the pace was different. Only three social workers saw very little difference between the Family Group Conference and other decision-making processes, and none of these had attended a Conference.

Over two thirds said that they thought the model could empower families, with the rest saying yes, but giving various qualifications. The qualifications involved debates about what empowerment means: whether it stems from giving families choice or from giving them information, whether it implies they have all the power or have their strengths and resources recognised in a more empowering way. Taking these debates into account all the social workers thought that the Family Group Conference is more empowering for families than the current child protection conferences or review meetings.

Most social workers wanted the model to remain available, with over half hoping that it would be expanded and become better resourced. A small number were indifferent, and about a fifth were reserving judgement until experience or evaluation provided more information.

We also asked social workers what concerns they had about the model. These largely related to the expectations the model placed on families. There were doubts about whether families could overcome their suspicions of social services to participate, and about whether they could come together amicably to hear the information and to focus on the needs of the child. Other concerns related to the expectations the model placed on the social services. There were worries that the model might raise family expectations about resources available, and that it needed extra resources to implement, both in staff time and co-ordinator expenses. As we shall see these worries were not borne out by the results of the project. Finally there was a minority of social workers (a quarter) who had no worries about the model itself, but were anxious that it should continue and should not be reduced or disbanded. They were clear that it should be evaluated fairly in comparison with the reality of other approaches, which did not receive such close research attention, and that it should get managerial support to be resourced properly – without these changes they felt a good model might be burdened with unrealistic expectations.

Interviews with professionals who had attended a Family Group Conference give a picture of workers generally endorsing the model, sometimes with considerable enthusiasm. Thomas (1994: p. 10) reports social workers describing a 'feeling of elation' on using it. Staff who were initially sceptical were able to see the benefits of the model, and even where the outcomes were unclear, staff reported feeling that they and the family had gained from having participated in the process (Barker & Barker, 1995: p. 19). Lupton and her colleagues found professional information givers positive, with only one negative comment about the basic principles of the model. Criticisms were made of particular aspects of particular meetings, more often relating to the difficulties of involving other agencies than of working with the families (1995: pp. 83–85).

Thus almost all the respondents acknowledged the model's difference, its potential for empowerment and its worth in their district. This seems to be a very strong endorsement of the model from practitioners, although, as we have seen, it is somewhat truer in theory rather than in practice. The concerns help explain our finding that about a third of social workers chose not to use the model, and point up how difficult it is for some social workers to change their work in this innovative way.

However, the model clearly affected the views of some staff, and as one put it: 'We won't make so many assumptions in future. We learnt from the situation'.

## Family members

Overall, family members were reported to be very positive about using Family Group Conferences. Lupton and her colleagues found that 86% thought it was 'very good' or 'good in parts', and elsewhere families were reported to feel that it was a 'natural' way to make decisions (Barker & Barker, 1995: p. 13). The benefits of 'bringing everything out in the open' were often quoted by family members, even though the difficulties of doing so were acknowledged. Barker and Barker report family members speaking very emotionally about their own lives and regrets, referring to instances within the family that had had lifelong adverse effects on them because 'upsetting things were not to be talked about' (1995: p. 9).

The interviews undertaken with family members did not specifically ask them to compare the Family Group Conference with other meetings they had attended. However, a number of family members did comment on this, comparing this model favourably, particularly with their own experiences of 'not knowing' or 'not being heard':

> 'When I was in care we had case conferences. We knew they were going on but couldn't go. Then we could go, and all these people I hardly knew, knew all these things about me. I'd bawl my eyes out. I would wonder what they were talking about as I was waiting to go in.'

Rosen reports one family who so preferred the format of the Family Group Conference in enabling their needs to be heard that they asked for similar procedures in their child protection review conference. The negative views generally held of child protection conferences (see for example Farmer & Owen, 1995: pp. 102–122) are not repeated for Family Group Conferences.

So would families use the model again? Researchers found that the meeting had been emotional and stressful for family members, but that the majority would choose to deal with future issues similarly. Where family members were given a hypothetical choice, to have a Family Group Conference or to have social services sort out a similar family problem in another way, just under three quarters preferred the Family Group Conference.

## Conclusions

The information we have gathered points up the fact that the Family Group Conference is very different in practical terms, and *feels* different to participants, when compared to other sorts of meetings. The difference stems from the principle that the meeting is for the family, it is *theirs*, rather than for the professionals. The independence of the co-ordinator is significant in maintaining the neutrality of the meeting, avoiding bias towards the professionals' or particular family members' agendas. The family *ownership* of the meeting leads to differences of venue, time and length, and to much greater involvement of parents, relatives and the young people themselves.

Participants are generally positive about the process of the Conference model both in the details of its management and its principles. Despite it being difficult for them in different ways, professionals and family members alike think it is worthwhile and would want the model to continue to be available.

# Chapter 7

# Co-ordinators' Work

We have given an overview of the co-ordinators' role in previous chapters; this chapter describes their work in all of its complexity. It does so by using our interviews with them to allow the story of the Conferences to emerge. We have used the co-ordinators' own words to try to give a real feeling of the Conferences. This approach has been taken because of the difficulty of conveying just how different the Family Group Conferences are, and the problems of trying to present data that encompass 80 unique events. It is easy to equate Conferences with existing meetings and processes, to which a few more family members are invited. But there is a qualitative difference, and the role of the independent co-ordinator is very important in establishing this difference. We looked for a new way of presenting these qualitative differences, and acknowledging the wide range of experiences that arise from the unique individual Conferences taking place within their common frame.

We are therefore going to let the co-ordinators tell their *travellers' tales*, using the headings of the Rough Guide to co-ordinating Family Group Conferences given in Chapter Three. We then present some examples within the theatre metaphor which was also suggested in that chapter, as an illustration of this multi-faceted role.

## Experiences of the 'Rough Guide' traveller

The words below are, with the exception of linking sentences and liberties of punctuation, those of the co-ordinators in the study explaining how they went about their work. They provide a form of case study, or case studies, of the work of the co-ordinators, as they struggled to develop practice from principles, in the pressurised world of the families and services that they were trying to help.

### Who is in the family?

#### Making the first contact

How much do I want to be told and how much do I want to find out for myself about conflicts in the family? It may be better not to follow the social worker type approach which is to gather as much information as possible beforehand. As a co-ordinator I don't need to know a lot of information about the family, what I need is the key concern about the family, the issue that social services is concerned about. But it's absolutely crucial that if social services know that there's any chance of any violence then they must tell me. I was totally unprepared for one father. Afterwards the social worker said 'Oh, yes. He physically put me out of the house once'. If I'd known that before when I met him the first time I would have maybe handled it differently.

Contacting the family in the first place can be a real nightmare. Often, after the first contact, the order in which I see people is more due to practical considerations than to choice. I phone up a load of people and it's who can see me first really. Its a matter of who I can fit in or if they can fit me in. The first one I did I remember ringing three times and just not getting anybody answering the phone and then writing and saying can you contact me and that worked. So I think sometimes you just have to leave it to the family to get back to you.

I'd always want the close family members to know first about the Family Group Conference and discuss it, but exactly who to start with depends on the way in which you work as a co-ordinator and the way the family expresses itself. It's very difficult to know beforehand, before meeting them, who's the best person to start with. The first thing I do is try to explain what Family Group Conferencing is all about and I'll tell what I know at that stage, what the social worker has told me, and they'll say 'that's not how I see it', so I start to compile a family agenda. They might be saying 'well the social worker is crap really, that's the problem', so that will be on the agenda.

It was a major problem having to do everything by mail, what I did in the end was lots of ad hoc visits to the mum on the off chance that she'd be in and nine times out of ten, it might have been as much as that, she wasn't. As it happened she lived in a block of flats where you had one of those coded things, so there was no letter box so I couldn't even put a note through the letter box because there wasn't one. I think I got in once with the postman and left a little note under the door. With another family I sent them a letter and their boxes were outside and somehow they didn't get it because the letter was stuck in there. So I was passing there one day and I thought I should drop in and see this family, so I dropped in. Now he was annoyed, he said to me 'why didn't you send us notice that you were coming', so I said I did. Anyhow I was lucky. She said 'no you didn't' and I said 'well I put it in the letter box' and she went out and it was stuck in the letter box so she came in and apologised. But he was very hostile. He said 'who is in charge of you, I want to know your manager, I want to know your director's name' and that sort of process. Anyway his younger brother who was more calm and collected explained to him that it wasn't my fault, I was just carrying out my duty and then he calmed down a little.

*Identifying and negotiating*

I met the teenage girl and spent the time just trying to find out who was important to her, and who the family was. Often it's a friend from school or somebody we wouldn't have thought of inviting, or a neighbour who they want to support them. Then key people in the young person's day to day care will point in a direction and then it's rather like a rolling stone gathers moss. If other members of the family have said 'well so and so should be invited' then I think I need to go back and check out with mum or the young person to make sure that's safe, that there's no history with this particular relative of anything that the young person is feeling unpositive about.

The father was completely unhappy about his mother, the grand-mother, coming, because he felt that she'd never looked after him, never cared for him. So we had to have quite a big debate about the fact that actually she was still in touch with them and that they row a lot and it was not going to be helpful to come up with a plan that she didn't know about and that he hadn't agreed with her because it might fall apart. So we had to do a lot of negotiating. I just said 'what do you think would happen if she didn't come? Or if she did?'. So we explored what would happen and the dad agreed that he thought it was okay to contact her.

Then there were a number of relatives who the girl didn't want to come to her Conference. She thought that they would just spread family gossip around and make life very difficult for her. I did a lot of work with her to try and see if there was a way in which they could be invited or how they could get their views in because I thought that they would actually be very good people to have at the meeting. But she was clearly saying that if she came and saw them there she would leave. So in that particular case I didn't invite them.

## Getting them there

I think people are willing to see you and find out what it's all about. I find that even before I get there they know what it's about, it's almost like a jungle drum syndrome. One person remembers 'Oh yes there's Uncle David down in Southampton' and you get the address. By the time I phone a day or two later they say 'oh yes come down, so and so did tell me you would be phoning'. So they had already been contacted and forewarned. I don't think I've ever gone to anybody who really had no idea why I was there.

People seem to come once they realise that they really are being given the power to make decisions. It takes quite a long time for that to flower in their minds because it is still a very novel concept. And I think one can tend to hook people by saying that they are important, that people who are important and significant in the life of this young person are the people who are being asked, and their views are going to be welcomed. I think people tend to like that.

Also you look at the family and you look at the people that are very constructive and you try to hang onto those people because they are the ones that will make the Conference successful. I went to talk to the grandfather because it was becoming clear that he was a fairly dominant character in the family. I saw it as a cascade, hoping that if I got him on my side then he might be able to exert some influence.

Generally siblings do appreciate being involved and for their voice to be heard. I think people often try and protect them by not sharing what's happening but I think if you actually tell children what's happening they pick out the bits they understand and ignore the rest. I think they benefit from that, because they do sort of know. I had one where a sibling was in the States but felt very strongly about the process and I had a couple of conversations with her before the meeting and got her point of view which I presented to the meeting and then phoned back afterwards and let her know the outcome. So she was involved but at quite a distance.

## Keeping them out

I suppose I work from the principle that if someone is saying to me that they have an alcohol, drug or mental health problem and they're saying to me very clearly that they don't know whether they're going to be able to attend sober, or clean of drugs then I would think very strongly about not inviting them. The same if they were particularly violent or abusive. But I will explore how they can get their views into the meeting. Is there a cousin who is going to be invited that could speak on their behalf? Or maybe they could write a letter? So they're not totally excluded, but they are not actually physically present on the day.

Nobody was excluded from the one I did except the grandfather. During the conversation it turned out that the two daughters had been abused by him and he was kept away in the other bit of the house, and already they'd policed themselves. Also the mother didn't want to invite her brother-in-law who had really invited himself, and I very much went along with that because she said he was a waste of space.

## Priority of efforts

If you are offering the family a service then you need to give them the time that they need to do it. If social services were rushing the family, if they felt they needed it in two weeks and the family weren't going to be ready for at least four weeks then really it's down to social services to hold back. It's the family's pace, it's the family's meeting, it'll be organised at their pace at their request. Now where that gets difficult is if there's any court action pending with the family. Very often we would want to get a Conference in so that we could take the plan to court. Now that benefits the family, so families will rally to that because it's in their interest.

I think it is more difficult working with the professionals than it is with family members. The family members seem to understand the idea of the Conference much easier than other professionals. I always see the professionals as well and talk through with them what kind of thing should be included in the report. I prepare them by saying to them, 'well the family may question you about what you're saying, how would you deal with that ... this is the family's meeting, you are going to the family's meeting to present information'. I always give them the option that either they can go through the report with the child or parents concerned or alternatively they can send it to me a week before the meeting so I can go through it, so that the family knows what's going to happen. I think only one person has asked *me* to do it, everyone else has done it themselves prior to the meeting, which I think is the right way to do it.

Another big thing at that point is that there's often been a lengthy history with social services and the social worker often carries around all that disappointment and history of the family and doesn't really think that this family can change anyway, so it's trying to forget a lot of the past and concentrate on the present. So if the social worker will be thinking about the present and not the past, then we've got the chance of getting some plan that everyone will accept. I have had long conversations with social workers about wished-for outcomes in terms of what's practical, what's realistic, what can be resourced, what's available. It's their job to make sure in stage one that they've been clear about that to the family group.

I think sometimes teachers find it a bit difficult because they're used to being in an authority role as well as facilitating. There have been difficulties with psychiatrists, doctors, as they tend to have a very different view of things and the way things are done and so there's a lot of hard work that goes in with them. Sometimes you think that the psychiatrists or doctors have understood what you've said to them and then they go and do something really difficult to believe. A psychiatrist, after I met with him, he then wrote a letter to the family members which was going to destroy the whole meeting. You know, the language he used in the letter, the kinds of things he was saying, if that letter had got to the child I think it really would have destroyed the whole thing.

## Engaging the family

### Successes

The social worker said 'she'll never come'. I said 'she might, it can happen'. I did all I could. I gave her my home number so she could ring me any time. I said 'I understand this is very, very painful but I also think it's important for you to be there in order to influence this decision-making. That's really important and we need you to be there. However, I can't make you come, but I will do anything I can to make it easier for you. Bring a friend if you like. If it helps for me to sit beside you I will do that. I will come and get you and walk you there if you like'. But she wasn't having any of that and she came on her own.

There was one where it was a question of one saying 'I won't come if he comes' and the other saying 'I won't come if they come'. I spent a lot of time talking about the reasons for them coming, why it was important for them to be there. I said that it was because the young person concerned wanted them to be there, they belonged to the wider network, and that was a good enough reason. I also spent as long trying to be empathic to how they would feel. I said 'look of course I understand that in your eyes this guy's a complete bastard and he is as far as you are concerned, but we're putting that to one side for the purpose of this meeting. That's big people stuff and you have to deal with that in big people's ways, but at the moment what that's doing is it's having an effect on what's going to happen to a young person who does not have that power. It's not their problem that there's problems at this level, so we just have to put that on ice.'

Contacting the father was an interesting experience because I actually think the girl felt that he wouldn't come because (she didn't actually say it like this) 'he's not interested in me any more'. On the surface it looked a bit like that, she hadn't seen him for three months, there was no kind of regular contact at all. He was obviously getting on with his own life running a business somewhere about a hundred miles away, and so there was obviously not much rapport there. On the other hand once I had communicated with him – I had to do two letters, several phone calls, mobile phone, you know all this stuff – and eventually he agreed to come. I didn't think he would but he did come and it was a significant element of the Conference.

Another girl wanted her step-father there. She called him dad, but he'd now split up. Her mother was saying 'I'm not going if he's there', it was one of those. And she also wanted his parents there. So I supported her in that. It took a while to persuade everybody that that was okay, that they could hack that, that they would manage, and that there were good reasons for it. And that was it.

## Failures

Everyone said about the dad 'oh he won't come' but I wanted to invite him, so I wrote him a letter. I didn't get a reply but the person he was living with opened the letter and rang me to say he wasn't there and gave me the phone number of the pub he was living in. I couldn't get hold of him however hard I tried. I rang at six o'clock in the morning and eight o'clock at night and I left messages with the landlord who said that the dad had got the message. So I assume he just didn't want to know, which was sad. The mum only had a father alive. I did write to him and he made it clear through a message he left for me that he wanted nothing to do with his daughter or the situation. On the day of the Conference I actually called round at his house to make absolutely sure that that was what he meant and he wasn't in, so there was nothing more I could do.

One young person wanted both her father and her mother there. In the end the mother wouldn't come basically because the father was coming. But maybe it was also a reflection of where she was in her commitment to the daughter as much as trying to avoid conflict.

### Using advocates and supporters

I think the use of an advocate is crucial. If the pattern of the family has been to silence the young person then they're going to try that again. I think one can try and overcome that in the beginning by emphasising that it's a meeting for the child and that everybody needs to be heard including the child. I usually actively explore with people who seem a bit fragile about the whole thing who is going to support them in the meeting. So I suppose as it starts to become clearer to me that there are some people who are feeling really hopeless, if people start saying there's no point in me coming because I'm not going to be able to say something, then I'll start thinking with them, 'Well how could we make that better for you? Is there something we can do differently in the meeting? Is there somebody in the family who helps you say things? Or is there somebody that you've got around out there who might help you a bit?'.

The child can choose a person right outside the family, someone at school. Then you are putting that person in a difficult situation because you are sort of launching them into a family where it could become quite volatile so you need to be around for them too to check that they're all right. In one Conference two friends of the girl were invited and only one came. The other one would have been a good advocate but her parents didn't want her to be involved. But the other one's parents were fine, they were supportive. In the end the friend came and the girl herself didn't, but he was in there and he played an active part. He was only eleven but he clearly played an active part, he was doing things on the flip chart. When it came to putting the plan into a more articulate form I made a point of checking out with him how he thought the girl might view that.

After all the work engaging them I give them a call maybe two days, three days before the Conference just to make sure everything's going OK and there's not going to be any difficulties. I also try to send the agenda out to people before they come so they've had a while to look at it. But even then I think it really is up to the family at the end of the day whether they attend or not.

## *Practicalities*

The logistics of bringing everybody together can be quite frustrating. They'll ring you to say 'I checked it out with Uncle Bill and he can be there but he can't be there until after six and Aunty Betty's coming from X but can she have the train fare', so all that sort of thing is going on all along as well; it's constant checking out in the same way that you do with any other case, you're just doing it with family members.

### *The venue*

I was looking for a place to hold it and the teenage aunt took me to the person who managed the local village hall and I booked it there and then on the spot. I paid for it out of my own money and got it back eventually, ten quid there on the table.

In the family time I could hear these raised voices, and all the other people using the building were saying 'what's happening?'. They couldn't hear what was being said but just all these raised voices. I thought I'll never hold it here again, it'll have to be a room with no other people around. Then the only other problem was that there was a lot of noise because there was a pneumatic drill or generator or something outside. Fortunately the workmen were prepared to stop for the duration of the Conference.

### *Date and time*

I've done a lot of my conferencing in the evening from six onwards. While we are encouraged to offer people loss of earnings it's often that it's not about earning, it's about commitments they've got at work. Especially with people like aunts and uncles that are sometimes peripheral, you don't know how important they are going to be when they get there. I think they sometimes feel awkward about accepting money for coming whereas they would have come after work. So I would encourage them to have it after work, because I think that what they're doing is important.

We had a bit of backwards and forwards about the final time that everyone could make because one person had to come by bus from the other side of London and one couple had to come up from Surrey and didn't want to come in the rush hour, and the kids had to be got to school and nursery.

### *Transport*

If people haven't got transport I make sure I send them a train ticket or whatever so they are not actually out of pocket to come to the meeting. I do offer those expenses anyway, and I always say I'll send you a train ticket and we'll make sure there's a taxi to take you from the train station to wherever. I have to pay it myself and then I claim it back. So it means you have to have quite a lot of money with you as well.

Three family members came down from the north of England and I don't think they really would have been able to do that unless we were able to pay their fares. Then I send out letters with maps explaining how to get there if need be, places they can park if they are driving.

### Food

I always ask if there's access to a kettle and cups and I bring tea, coffee, juice, biscuits. I always leave the kettle in there so people can make themselves tea and coffee and there's biscuits there. I've never had to provide food, the meetings have never been that long.

Well I've done all sorts. Sandwiches and sausage rolls, finger food. We've sent out for pizzas. I've done it myself here, quiches and sausages. I've done soup and bread and cheese and whatever. Most of the time I do it but I get help, voluntary from a member of the team who doesn't happen to be doing very much and will nip out in the morning or whatever. It feels hard trying to juggle it all.

### Child care

We've employed people that have been sessional workers for the borough and people who've done odd bits of work, a foster carer that sort of thing, just employed on an hourly rate. Other times we haven't actually had anybody and I just made sure there were some toys around and we just worked through that. That's just a question of making sure that nobody's bothered about the kids being there and working it out in a child friendly way.

### Fitting the role in with other work

I visited family members at the weekend – particularly the ones that were in the north of England, I actually went up there over the weekend. If you are trying to set things up in a couple of weeks and you've got two or three evenings to spare you just blitz those evenings. Then I give people my number at work. That's okay except that people there aren't used to dealing with clients, so when they've had the mother ringing up in a complete state, and various other members of the family ringing, they've actually found that quite difficult to cope with.

## Clear information and chairing the meeting

I have flip chart pages with the process of the Conference written on them up on the wall before they come in the room, and also one with just the child's name on so that they can keep focused on the child. At the beginning you need to have quarter of an hour where people are settling in, they make each other cups of tea, it's all just kind of hospitable stuff, they haven't seen each other for ages so there is a bit where everybody in the family does need the time to say, hello, how are you, how was your journey.

If I ask a particularly dumb question it often encourages the family, it's almost a way of indicating it's okay to ask. For instance in one the family were initially fairly passive about it but then they began asking quite pertinent questions of both the teacher and the policeman.

One of the difficulties is keeping the boundary between the family having an opportunity to ask the professionals questions and them starting to come in with their comments and feelings while the professionals are still there.

## Moving to the family session

Often before I've left the room I'll leave up the list of questions again as a way of offering focus. They might be 'what sort of accommodation would be right for this child?' 'By when should that be arrived at?'. Just getting them to think about the detail really. The more detail there is in the plan the more it's likely to work. And I get them to think about who they want to present their plan back to social services when they have finished.

Then I leave them, letting them know where I'm going to be so that they can come and get me if they get stuck or if they want any more information or whatever else I can help with. Otherwise they can just get me at the end.

## Practising respect

You can't know what goes on in families can you? I'm sure there was an awful lot going on that I wasn't aware of. I think it works better if there's a larger family particularly if people come in who haven't been seen to have a role in the situation before. If there's been one rather dominant person in the family, I think that can sometimes be balanced by having uncles or aunts there.

I've found myself (perhaps more in the third one because you get more experienced and know that families can cope with it all right) allowing families to referee their own affairs. Thinking about the last one where the dad was pretty abrasive in his style and a bit curt and dismissive of other people's ideas, one side of me wanted to come in and say 'well I think it would be a good idea if people respect each other a bit more'. I could have said that, but the family did that. The family did it their own way and set the tone while we, the professionals, were there. So I just leave them with the simple ground rules, although I've seen how by the time I've left after an hour or so, families have been capable of setting their own ground rules.

Dad's an example of someone who came with some reluctance, he had some pretty authoritarian views as to how he could sort it all out. But even in the initial stages it was quite clear that the family weren't going to sit there and let him pontificate on his authoritarian stance and were going to say 'it's a bit more complicated than that'.

One really made me think a lot about what on earth are we doing to young people in this process. In a way that meeting had to be stopped because it got that painful for the young person. But what she said was that it was stuff she needed to hear, it was stuff she was aware of anyway. So there's the element of wanting to protect people from what they know anyway. But then that's the thing about the process, the process was only reflecting what was going on in that child's family every day.

## Dealing with the unexpected

I feel by the time the meeting's started it's beyond my control. I haven't actually had anyone walk out. I have had people not turn up. I usually put it back to the family and they say 'oh we'll just go ahead'. I came out of one Conference at one point just to sort out the tea and coffee or something and I saw the mother cruising up and down outside so I just played it really cool and said 'it's nice to see you, listen we're just having coffee now, why don't you . . .' and just sort of made it seem as if it was entirely normal.

In another one the mother actually came on time and while we were waiting to see if anyone else was going to turn up she left. She walked out. She said she was going to the shop and she was gone about forty five minutes or so. She did come back when none of us thought she would. Really we just got on with it, we felt that it was still important to consider the child even without the mother being there. I actually went out and walked up and down the streets looking for her and couldn't find her. She said that she was finding it very hard and needed some space and that was fair enough. She joined back in and was glad that they had continued.

Then the teenager didn't turn up. I think that was quite a shock because I'd spoken to her the day before, she was very excited about coming and then she didn't come and none of us really expected that. I think it changed the focus of the meeting to how the family could support the child rather than thinking about how the child's behaviour could be different.

I've also had people turn up that I didn't know were coming. I had one chap who I'd never even seen or heard of before and he came. That took me back a bit, but it was okay.

*In the family time*

More than one person has walked out with either tears pouring down their faces or gasping that they have just not been able to stand the pressure. It can be really, really painful. I've just maintained my cool, because whatever is happening it is important for them to manage and I've just waited. I don't know if they are going to go back in or not, but so far they always have.

The adolescent girl would pop out for two or three minutes saying 'oh it's a bit boring just now, I'll just come out here', so obviously when things were a bit difficult she would just come out.

## Clarifying agreements

The general problems that I've found with their plans is they're not specific enough and I'll say maybe you need to think about this some more. I just go in with a different coloured pen and say 'well, when you say Michael has got to go and live with aunt, do you mean straight away? Do you mean he is going to be paying rent? Is he expected to be under curfew? Are there house rules and does he know them? What would count as a successful period? When do you think we need to look at it to see if it's failed or not? How are we going to protect the aunt from maybe being exploited or feeling abused or taking on too much responsibility – who's going to support her?'.

It is difficult because as far as they are concerned they've done it. I can remember having to shout above the din to try to get it clear. The thing is, they say they know what they mean. Just like social workers know what they mean when they're talking to clients but the clients don't know: this is the reverse.

I always check that everybody is in agreement with what's being said because I'm very aware that some people in families are very much stronger than others. Sometimes people say 'I'm not in agreement with that bit, but I'll accept it' and that has to be noted as well.

I've had one Conference which got really stuck; they simply reached an impasse. So they called me back in and I said 'There's several things we could do. One is we can just abandon today's event, reconvene and have another go later. Or we can abandon absolutely now and say we reached no outcome. Or we can fashion up some sort of compromise and do it as a trial period and them come back and review the outcome', which was indeed the one they took to in the end. So in the end I helped them do a deal.

## Monitoring

It's generally been the social worker because there's nobody else to do it. Well there's nobody to check out whether the social worker does review it or not, is there? I have actually talked with the family about the process of making a complaint if they were to feel that they weren't receiving the service.

I think that the family group themselves must be responsible for deciding who's going to figure out whether the plan worked or not, and what constitutes a failure or success and who's in charge of that. In a sense that's going on anyway. In all the families the problems are going to be such that somebody somewhere is going to continue to be concerned and involved.

## Thinking of the Conference as a special, theatrical event

We provided in Chapter 3 a metaphor for the Conferences as a form of theatrical event, with a cast, a setting and a plot with attendant ad-libs. The co-ordinator is something of a director, a set designer and a facilitator at the writers' workshop that is developing the script. Like any analogy it should not be taken too far, but we give below some of the ways that it may provide an additional insight into the work of the co-ordinator.

### Leading actors

I arrange to see them on the telephone and then I go and visit them and sometimes when I'm there I'll arrange when I'll come again because I feel it's really important to keep the parents informed and if the child is old enough, to keep the child informed of what is happening, who am I now seeing, what do they think about this. Also I think it's quite important to be able to talk with them about who's not coming, because that's quite hurtful sometimes because they feel quite rejected when people start saying 'I'm not coming'.

But first I'd sort out with mum if she wants to tell the family members or if she doesn't want to say anything and I'll do all that. I need to be clear who's doing what because she might say 'well, don't contact my sister, I'll do that' or she might want to check that it's all right to give me their addresses because of the way people feel about social services. So there's a bit of a time lapse there because of giving people time to tell me how they want me to do it. When it's the carer that doesn't want particular people to come because they have never helped, they've never done anything, it's 'why let them get away with it – this is an opportunity where they're going to be put on the spot and they might have to do something' say in terms of absent dads. That often works to get them invited. In one, to get the father involved we had a telephone link in a prison so that they could talk and get his views and so on, which was very good.

The social workers do wonder how they are going to be received, wondering if the family are going to come down on them really hard in the meeting and sometimes they do. They'll say 'We're very angry with what you've done, we don't think you should have done it that way, you should have asked us.' But it also gives the social worker the opportunity to say, well, I'm doing it now, I really want this for you, I want you to have this space'.

I believe if the social worker has a negative view and doesn't want the process to go through, this causes a lot of problems. In order for a Family Group Conference to work properly the social workers need to be welcoming of it.

### Bit players

When I went to see the aunt she just came from prison. She did some shoplifting somewhere around here and when I went to meet her they said she is in the police station, so I went there. We went to the police station and we met there and I managed to talk to the sergeant in charge and they released her.

The family wanted to invite a family friend who was a solicitor, he'd been the family solicitor way back ... and social services were saying 'why do they want a solicitor, they can't have a solicitor, solicitors are people who aren't coming'. But the family were quite clear he was being invited because he was a family friend.

### Director

The only thing that would go wrong I guess would be if you get petty jealousies flaring up like 'oh I'm not taking part because you spoke to the wrong person first'. I would see it as part of my job to notice that and take care of it and make sure it's sorted.

I think it's important at the beginning of the Conference to go back over what it's about and that there's two parts. It's also important to make sure that people feel safe, that they will be listened to and establish a few ground rules about listening and that everybody needs a chance to speak, everybody needs a chance to feel that they've been listened to, rules about non-violence. If people are bringing along angry feelings then you need to acknowledge that. And you need to be sure that people know that there are places, somewhere they can go, that you are around if people do get stuck and what the boundaries are.

Then I was able to invite the professionals to speak. I was quite deliberate in the order of presentation. I decided to leave one particular professional till last because I wanted him to have the last word as it were.

After each information giving bit I make sure the family understand what's been said and if they've got any questions, but at the same time I also discourage them from starting to discuss the report, I always say to them 'that's perhaps something you can start discussing when you're on your own, but if there is something you would like clarified that's what this is for'. When that's finished and I'm absolutely sure everybody's clear what's been said, I ask the professional to leave.

I've actually found it very refreshing professionally ... I enjoy the business, that it has a beginning a middle and an end ... It challenges a bit of me which I like using best which is being imaginative and innovative and creative and trying to bring out the best in people.

### Set and lighting designer

I suggest to them that it is a neutral area, so I ask them because most of the time I don't know myself what's in that area and I sort of say is there any sort of church halls or community rooms or anything nearby where we can rent a room for a few hours. People are very helpful, they know what's in their local community really, so they pick the venue and the time.

I have to set out all the chairs, arrange the room the way I want it.

I'd had a bit of a think about it and I'd decided that we had two different sets of people coming really, professionals I mean: the people who were there to talk about the children and the people who were there to talk about the adults. I didn't actually feel it was appropriate for everybody to hear everything so I had a little waiting room for the professionals so we could do some sorting out.

### Stage fright problems

One social worker found it very hard to let the process happen, it was almost as if he was delaying the process a bit. There was stuff going on and he'd keep coming up with 'oh, what if...' and 'I'm worried about this' and ... I've learnt to recognise avoidance strategies and that's not an accusation at all, it was a very complicated situation and he was scared about what would happen when all that lot were gathered together. I think for him it was quite difficult, quite scary to take his hands off the wheel.

I guess I'm pretty underhand to tell you the truth. Like with family members 'Well don't you want to know what he's saying about you and if he goes to the Conference and you don't, how will you know what he's saying about you'. That's often got people there. and 'Are you going to let this person take control or do you want some say in what's happening?' because often they'll say 'I'm not going, she's terrible he's terrible, they do this and they do that' and I'll say 'Well why don't you come and say this at the Conference'. I wonder myself if that's right but I haven't got another way of doing it.

I prefer to talk to the family first before the professionals arrive. We start off and get the agenda up and I try to find somebody that will be the scribe so 'who's going to do this, who's the teacher in the family?' – we usually have a little giggle about that ... so that sort of thing lightens it up.

The grandma ... she was okay but every other day she was ringing up ambivalent about the whole idea, partly because she might be under criticism as well. There were times when she phoned me every other day in the ten days before the Conference, once we'd fixed the date, nearly always saying 'I don't think it's a good idea' when we started the conversation and by the end of the conversation saying 'all right we'll try it out then'.

What I've found is that people fear the conflict more than the reality of the conflict. Sometimes people have told me 'if you invite all of us, you do realise there's going to be some blood flow' and 'you do realise it's going to be disastrous' 'it will be terrible' it will be frightening' and in fact it hasn't been. People have been more restrained than that, although people have brought a lot of anger to the meeting and you do need to acknowledge that and allow that to be recognised at the beginning. I think in most cases people's fears and fantasies of the conflict have been worse than they actually are.

### Consequences of losing the plot

The step-dad just said 'I shall make sure nobody goes' and that was generally his attitude. Initially the relatives were saying yes, yes, we'll come and then when you checked back with them later on with the date it was no no we're not coming now. He was quite open about it and said 'I've had a word with so and so and I've told them they're not coming' and that was it. It was really difficult. Two of the relatives said they would come and I ordered a taxi to pick them up to take them to the meeting: they didn't come. I phoned the taxi firm and they said when they turned up they were told they were no longer needed. So the only people who turned up were the parents.

What I do while the professionals are talking is to actually write up what I think they are asking of the family ... so once they leave I've got this list.

Knowing that there was a real possibility of conflict at least between father and mother, I wasn't at all sure how I was going to be able to cope with that.

### Effect of different theatres on the same play

I should have visited the hotel beforehand, we were in the corner of a huge room which wasn't very appropriate.

I got a lot of stick afterwards because everybody in this family smoked and it was a very non-smoking church environment. The alternative would have been ... actually the local community centre might have been okay but that particular place is like a drinking club and two members of the family had drink problems so it was just a no-go area and they accepted and understood that.

Then there's a whole complicated thing about hidden agenda and what they all know but are not going to talk about. In this last one it dawned on me that there was a whole hidden area to do with the wife's health.

*Impact of ad-libs*

Sometimes if I've thought it might be hard for them ... I've left a list of rules. There was one where ... I actually wrote this on a poster on the wall. Think of what you are going to do as a jigsaw and everybody has got a piece to say, don't interrupt each other.

The friend wasn't there by this point so I rang him up and he was actually in tears on the other end of the phone saying he didn't think he could come because he just couldn't bear to be there because he just couldn't see any other way that was going to happen than the children to come into care and he couldn't bear to see that happen. When I told the family about that of course it had quite an impact.

There was a lot of shouting in the family time and I thought 'Oh god, will I go in there and make sure everyone's okay?'. I had to really make myself hope that if someone's not all right they would come and get me. When I went in there it was very obvious that one or two of them had been very, very upset. They didn't share with me anything that had been said but they just came up with this plan which was the best plan ever I think.

# The co-ordinators' conclusions

It's wonderful actually seeing families being empowered and taking responsibility, and not just the immediate family but the extended family. Especially to see them come up with a plan that will work, that social services would never have been able to come up with if there had not been a Family Group Conference. Also, I've really enjoyed being able to do work in my own way but within the framework of the Family Group Conference scheme and getting a group of people together and conveying to each other 'we're all equal here ... we're all here on the same level of importance and everybody's view is of equal value'. I hold that quite strongly as a philosophy of life.

It's been very exciting seeing families becoming empowered and making their wishes known, finding that there's more resource within a family than they thought there was anyway, finding that they do have a voice and it is listened to. Also it's exciting being in on something new, it's good to do a bit of pioneering work.

# Chapter 8

# Outcomes

In this chapter we look at the outcomes of the Family Group Conferences under study. We are seeking to answer questions such as: Did the families make plans, and if so, what sort of plans? Were the social workers satisfied that the plans met the needs of the child, including providing adequate protection? What might have happened to these children if they had not had a Family Group Conference? How do the outcomes compare with those from other studies? Did the Family Group Conference process have any other outcomes for the participants unrelated to the actual plan made?

## The plans

Of the 80 Family Group Conferences we studied, 74 produced agreed plans addressing the needs of the child that were acceptable to the professionals and to the family members. In no instance was a plan rejected outright by the social services, and in cases where plans were taken back to child protection conferences or to court for ratification, this was achieved without difficulty.

In fact all but two Conferences were able to make plans of some sort. Three had some difficulties with planning but reached a consensus on the way forward: one agreed that the social worker should make the decision; one agreed a plan but reservations were expressed; one made a short-term plan but agreed to let the court decide the longer term plan. In a fourth case, very different from any of the others we looked at (Case 1, outlined below), it was those with parental responsibility who rejected plans made by other family members. Here issues of parental responsibility, working in 'the best interests of the child' and the wisdom of holding meetings without crucial family members being present are all raised.

Two Conferences failed to reach any agreement. In one the parents denied information relating to neglect, so there was no agreed agenda for decision-making, and the case went to court. In the other, the family met but were unable to resolve the issues and became too distressed to continue their discussions. Both of these cases were amongst the first few to be held, and both in fact were in the area which initially had categories of obligatory referral to the project. It is possible that in a different project these families would not have been considered suitable for the model; but it is also possible that with more experience, the staff could have prepared the participants or presented the information more effectively, and obtained better outcomes.

## Case 1

Two Family Group Conferences were held for a 12 year old girl, who was in foster care at the request of her family. The background was that the mother and step-father had rejected the girl, not allowing her any contact with her half brothers and sisters or with members of the family. The Conference was organised to seek alternatives to foster care. The step-father was very domineering, and the co-ordinator spoke of him as a very threatening and aggressive man, who very deliberately affected family attendance at the Conferences.

The first Conference was attended by paternal step-grandfather, maternal grandmother, two maternal cousins and a family friend. The step-father, and the mother, refused to meet with these relatives, and put ten other relatives off attending. However, the family that did meet produced a comprehensive plan, the step-grandfather and one of the cousins agreeing to share the care of the young person. They agreed to help her contact her parents if she wished and to maintain contact with other family members.

As those with parental responsibility had not attended, social services felt they could not follow the plan. A second Conference was held to which no family members other than the parents came because the step-father had, as he put it, 'made sure' they would not attend. The parents would not approve the family's first plan, and repeated their wish that the girl be looked after by the state, with agreement to gradually build up contact. Contact with other family members would be arranged by the parents, the girl was not to contact them herself. The social worker was hoping that this plan would lead to a reunion, and the plan was agreed.

Not long after the Conference the girl's foster placement broke down and she went to live in the residential children's home, where she remained without any contact with her parents at all. The co-ordinator appreciated the difficulties of the case, but felt that the first plan could have been acted on as being in the best interests of the child, and that the girl had been failed by the system.

## Content of plans: what did the families agree?

The families drew up plans that they thought met the needs of the child or young person: what services did they ask for, and what resources did they find from within the family?

### Services requested

We have grouped the services that were requested in the plans under the four areas of social services, health services, education and other agencies (Table 8.1). The most frequent pattern of request was for support from the social services: only six plans did not request social services help. The help requested was more often for counselling or support than for financial or practical assistance. This seems to be similar to the components of social work service offered to parents after child protection conferences (Thoburn *et al.*, 1995: p. 147), with the exception that families do not ask for 'advice', and are less likely to ask for a 'supportive relationship': perhaps these are more likely to be sought from family members.

For 24 families help from social services was the only resource requested. A further 46 families asked for social services resources in conjunction with help from other agencies, most commonly education and/or health. Three plans requested help from agencies other than social services and three plans did not request any outside resources at all. The detailed content of the remaining two plans was not available to us.

Requests for multi-agency resources in Family Group Conference plans appear to be broadly similar to those included in plans made at child protection conferences (Thoburn *et al.*, 1995: p. 140), as outlined in Table 8.2. However, comparing our information with decisions made at child care review meetings (Grimshaw, 1996), the Family Group Conference plan is considerably more likely to involve a wider number of agencies (Table 8.3). Family members therefore seem able to plan for different aspects of the child's needs, despite the fact that there are usually only one or two professionals present to give information to the family.

It is clear from the plans that families usually do want help, and are able to identify what they need. The Family Group Conference does not avoid the use of services; indeed it may involve a wider range of services than other kinds of meeting, and use those services differently. This may disappoint those who had hoped the model would enable family support to replace professional support, but reassure those worried that families might want to 'go off on their own'.

### Family resources

In addition to requests for service resources, almost all the family

**Table 8.1** Services requested at Family Group Conferences.

|  | *n* |
|---|---|
| **1. From Social Services** | |
| Social services not mentioned in plans | 6 |
| Time resource: | |
| counselling/family work | 11 |
| visit/support regularly | 10 |
| monitor/review | 9 |
| information/advice | 5 |
| change social worker | 4 |
| supervision/contact | 4 |
| assessment of carer | 2 |
| assessment of risk | 1 |
| Financial resource: | |
| regular small payment (e.g. for contact) | 9 |
| regular care/respite payment | 8 |
| one off payment (e.g. bedding, car seat) | 6 |
| shared specialist placement costs | 2 |
| provision of playscheme/holiday | 2 |
| foster care (permanent) | 5 |
| foster care (temporary) | 6 |
| new resid accom placement | 2 |
| continuing resid accom placement | 2 |
| **2. From Health** | |
| Health not mentioned in plans | 44 |
| Health visitors help | 10 |
| Adult counselling | 5 |
| Medical assessment/check up | 5 |
| Drink/drug services | 6 |
| Adult psychiatry info/help | 3 |
| Child guidance/child psychiatry | 7 + 1 discharge request |
| Residential psychiatry unit | 1 |
| Learning disability care | 1 |
| Occupational therapy help | 1 |
| Change of GP | 2 |
| **3. From Education** | |
| Education not mentioned | 51 |
| General support from school | 6 |
| Provide extra help | 5 |
| Help monitor children | 3 |
| Liaise with others | 3 |
| EWO help/involvement | 2 |
| Child to remain in school | 2 |
| Child to change school | 2 |
| Possible residential school place | 2 |
| Return to mainstream from special | 1 |

**Table 8.1** (continued)

|  | *n* |
|---|---|
| School to provide information | 1 |
| After school club | 1 |
| **4. From others** | |
| Other agencies not mentioned | 59 |
| Housing | 12 |
| Probation | 1 |
| Juvenile justice | 1 |
| Courts | 1 |
| Welfare/money advice | 1 |
| Voluntary agencies | 2 |
| Community groups | 2 |

**Table 8.2** Services requested in family plans and in child protection conference plans.

|  | FGC (%) | CPC (%) |
|---|---|---|
| SSD only | 31 | 42 |
| SSD and one agency | 36 | 26 |
| SSD and two or more agencies | 25 | 16 |
| No SSD but other agency | 4 | 2 |
| No agency resources | 4 | 8 |

**Table 8.3** Other agency involvement in plans made at Family Group Conference and review meetings.

|  | FGC (%) | Review (%) |
|---|---|---|
| Health | 42 | 15 |
| Education | 33 | 14 |
| Miscellaneous | 22 | 23 |

plans included resources from within the family. Only five made no mention of support or help to be given to the child or main carer by family members. The range of help offered by the family was wide, but was almost always of a practical nature. Sometimes it was a relative agreeing to telephone and keep in touch with the child; more often it was an offer of help in person, such as for babysitting, helping to clear the garden, sorting out the family finances, or taking the carer or the child out regularly. More onerous duties taken on included family members offering to care for children in emergencies, for weekends, holidays or full time. Almost a third of plans (31%) included family members taking on the care of the child(ren) concerned for some period of time. And it was not always relatives who took on this responsibility. In several instances it was a family friend or the child's peer's family, and in one case the adolescent boy's football coach. In two plans financial support was offered by the family: those with parental responsibility making private arrangements to pay family members offering to care for a child (Case 2).

## Case 2

This young girl lived with her mother and father until they separated. The father moved to live locally, and then when the girl was 13 she and her mother moved some distance away. The girl never really settled and at age 15 she ran away and made her way back to her home town, where she stayed in bed and breakfast accommodation. Her maternal grandparents took her in but were unable to offer a long-term placement for her. The Family Group Conference was called to establish a plan for the girl.

Present were the young person, the mother, the father, maternal grandmother and family friends consisting of a mother and daughter. The young person would not agree to inviting mother's cohabitee.

In the plan the family respected the girl's wish not to return to her mother's care. They agreed to a private fostering arrangement with the family friend, a financial support package to be negotiated between the two families. The girl also wished to return to her old school. The social services commented in the plans that they had a statutory duty to supervise private fostering arrangements, and that they could assist with a *placement agreement* between the family and the carer. They agreed to liaise with the school, and to meet the cost of a reconvened Family Group Conference.

In the event, the reconvened Conference did not take place because the situation was stable. The young person stayed with the family friend for a year, during which time she was getting 'support' from the social services department. She also disclosed that her mother's cohabitee had assaulted her. When her mother's relationship with this man broke up, the girl returned to her mother's care.

## Satisfaction with plans

### Professionals

The social workers, other professionals and co-ordinators we spoke to were generally very impressed by the plans the families had produced. Many made reference to the creativity of the plans, and the incorporation of ideas which social services would never have thought of. All of the plans produced were agreed by social services; none was thought to place the child or children at risk of significant harm.

Some plans were a considerable surprise to the professionals involved, and on occasion the Conference caused the social worker to change their mind about what was in the best interests of the child (Case 3).

## Case 3

A 15 year old girl had been 'looked after' for 10 years, and a Family Group Conference was convened to plan for her remaining 3 years in care. The co-ordinator had some difficulty in keeping the balance of the Conference towards the family because the people closest and most important to the young person were often professionals. Some relatives refused to attend, especially her mother and stepfather, and in the end her brother; her father, maternal aunt and uncle and an advocate friend did turn up. Also attending were her foster parents, her key worker and two representatives from school. An older sister who had also been in care was in America and was contacted by telephone: she sent her views to the meeting via the co-ordinator.

The social worker went to the meeting with the view that it would not be appropriate for the young person to go to live with her father, because of 'problems around dad'. However, this was the girl's expressed wish at the Conference, and the social worker came to the view that this was the most positive option for her. The father was willing to accept any support on offer from social services, and other family members agreed to keep in contact with her, despite some of them voicing reservations about the plan. The elder sister was informed of the plan by telephone later the same day, and asked for her concerns about the plan to be noted, with the added hope that the girl would get a lot of support.

The plan was implemented, the girl went to live with her father and this remained a successful placement.

Despite agreeing to the plans, it is perhaps not surprising that a small minority of social workers or other professionals involved were not completely happy with the plans resulting from the Conferences. Lupton and her colleagues (1995: p. 81) found that while the majority were satisfied or partly satisfied, two out of 24 were dissatisfied with the plans. Dissatisfaction was mostly due to the feeling that the family did not address all the issues of concern, even though they did produce plans that adequately protected or catered for the child's needs. Families may choose to limit their actions to those specifically connected with the problems presented at the Conference, and not to feel that this opens up other aspects of their life to examination and potential professional intervention. It is also important to note that this study was looking at the first 11 Family Group Conferences held in one project. It is possible that the information givers and co-ordinators learnt from this experience how to present their concerns better and set parameters for the plans, to enable the family to address the issues more fully. Barker and Barker (1995) found that the plans coming from the very early Conferences were criticised as being too vague and lacking 'necessary detail'. At later Conferences more time was spent in clarifying and agreeing the details of the plan, so that participants were clear about it. This process has already been described as one of the more difficult parts of the co-ordinator's role.

### Family

The majority of the 109 participating family members interviewed reported being positive about the plans made at the meeting, the figure being around 80% in all three studies available. Satisfaction at 4–6 months had fallen significantly in only a small percentage of the sample (12%) compared to satisfaction immediately after the Conference (Lupton *et al.*, 1995: p. 89). This was reported to be due to the difficulties experienced in implementation. That is, the content of the plan had been satisfactory but the implementation had not. We have tried to separate satisfaction with the plans themselves from opinions on their successful implementation.

## Were the plans expensive?

Many people feared that, given the chance, families would unreasonably ask for expensive services. Information on the plans was used to categorise them roughly into high, medium or low cost bands

High cost     =   those including residential or foster care.
Medium cost   =   those including continuing specialist services or other fairly substantial costs.

Low cost  =  those including one-off payments, ongoing small
             payments of under £10 per week, or an *ordinary*
             level of support services.

Three quarters of the plans were judged to be medium or low cost, and
in addition three plans did not cost anything as the family did not
request any outside services. Requests for financial support involved
one-off payments for basic domestic equipment, fares for contact or
boarding costs to carers. Requests for other types of service did not
seem to be exceptional. None of the social workers we spoke to thought
resource requests had been unreasonable. One complained that the
family had not made good or rapid use of the resources provided, but
several others commented that they would reasonably have expected
families to ask for more services. The families were not, then, 'greedy'
for services.

Further consideration of the costs is made later on in this chapter,
and we return again to this area in Chapter 9.

## Implementation

There are two ways of looking at the implementation of the plans. One
is to consider the details of the plan and whether everyone did exactly
what they said they would, and the other is to consider whether the
overall intent of the plan, for example to keep the child at home or to
provide a specialist placement, had been carried out successfully. We
have taken the more general view, asking 'was the overall intent of the
plan successfully implemented?'. We have done this for a number of
reasons. First, circumstances within families change and evolve over
time, so that what was an appropriate offer of help from, say, an aunt,
at the time of the Conference may not be appropriate six months later,
but other more appropriate help might be substituted that was not on
the family plan. In a detailed follow up it could look as if the aunt's part
of the plan had failed, even though the intent to provide help or support
had been maintained successfully.

Second, as many of the plans concerned actions to be taken by the
family members, follow up of the detailed implementation would
require a large number of interviews with family members. Apart from
the fact that we did not have the resources to carry out such a number
of interviews, the views of the potential actors and beneficiaries as to
what had actually been done could be expected to conflict at times. We
felt that we were not in a position to investigate these difficult but
interesting issues.

Our third reason for not looking at the detailed implementation was
that we did not have comparable information on the detailed implementation of plans made through other decision-making processes. For

instance, we do not know how many points of detail written into plans made at child protection conferences are carried out: do children receive the recommended regular medical checks? Are children referred to child psychiatry as planned and do they receive suitable treatment? Does the core group meet as often as planned? We felt that without comparable information, the family group process might be judged against a theoretical scale of success that bore no relation to the workings of the real world.

Recent research is providing some information on the plans made at review meetings (Grimshaw, 1996), where implementation relating to legal and placement decisions was found to be quite high at over 80%, but lower (45–60%) for *contact* and *miscellaneous* decisions. Implementation was rarely within set time scales, with only health decisions managing to be implemented in time in as many as one in five cases, and unplanned changes were frequent, with almost a third of contact decisions being affected. Taking these results to represent the *real world* of decision-making in social services, we should not perhaps have very high expectations regarding the implementation of Family Group Conference plans, especially as many of the decisions made at Family Group Conferences would fall into Grimshaw's categories of 'contact' and 'miscellaneous'.

### Implementation of Family Group Conference plans

The information we have regarding successful implementation of Family Group Conference plans is from the 'local evaluation' studies and from our own follow up of 80 of the 99 sample children over at least six months. These can be compared to Grimshaw's findings and also to the group of 19 child protection conferences studied by Lupton and her colleagues (Table 8.4). There are some difficulties in comparing these results, not least because different people are judging the success or otherwise of the plans. However, the data give a picture, albeit rather a hazy one, of Family Group Conference plans being successfully implemented at about the same rate as other plans. Family members were generally satisfied with the plan implementation.

## Outcomes

The outcomes information we obtained from social workers regarding the stability of the child's placement covered a year or more for all but 16 of the 80 children. For these 16 children we had 6 month outcome information. We have taken the stability of the planned placement to be one indication of the successful implementation of the overall intent of the plan.

In order to identify particular issues involved with Family Group

**Table 8.4** Comparison of implementation rates.

|  |  | (%) |
|---|---|---|
| Reviews (Grimshaw, 1996) | (*n* = 180) substantially or fully | 68 (range 45–84) |
| Child Protection Conference (Lupton *et al.*, 1995) | (*n* = 19) fully in social worker view | 66 |
| Family Group Conference (Lupton *et al.*, 1995) | (*n* = 13) wholly/mostly in majority family view partly in majority family view | 46 46 |
| Family Group Conference (Barker & Barker, 1995) | (*n* = 6) family group think plans being carried out | 83 |
| Family Group Conference (Rosen, 1994) | (*n* = 4) family group think plans being carried out | 75 |
| Family Group Conference (this study) | (*n* = 78) intent of plan, researcher rating | 75 |

*n* = number of meetings

Conference plans, and to compare the outcomes with those found by other researchers, the children we followed up were divided into groups according to the area of concern. We used three main groupings: those where the family was requesting accommodation, or where family breakdown was causing a real risk of accommodation; those for whom there were child protection concerns and those who were being looked after (not for child protection concerns).

We looked at the implementation and outcome of the placement plans for these three groups (Table 8.5). Stability of placement was generally high for all the children concerned. The group most susceptible to a change of placement plans in the 6 months or a year post Family Group Conference was the 'accommodation request/risk' group, where eight of the 21 children we followed up had a change of placement. Half of these remained within their family group but changed their place of residence. For example, in two cases the young person went to live with the father after the Conference but later returned to live with the mother (Case 4), and in another the shared care arrangement between the mother and a friend became a permanent placement with the friend. Family placements of the other four broke down, with each initially staying at their original residence but then moving into state care; three of these later moved back into the care of the family.

**Table 8.5** Placement plans carried out according to reason for concern.

|  | Accom risk (%) | Child protection (%) | Looked after (not child protection) (%) |
|---|---|---|---|
| Successful implementation | 61 | 83 | 81 |
| Situation changed but family negotiated resolution internally | 19 | 6 | 9 |
| Plan implemented but did not work | 19 | 6 | 9 |
| Plan not implemented at all | 0 | 6 | — |
|  | (n = 21) | (n = 35) | (n = 11) |

n = number of children

## Case 4

The 14 year old boy at the centre of this Conference had been leading an unsettled life. His mother and father had separated, and the boy remained with his mother, with whom he had a good relationship. The mother then became a Jehovah's Witness, and wanted him to go from door to door with her. This was very much resented by the boy, who started to run away, often staying with his maternal grandmother, sometimes elsewhere. The mother in turn resented him staying with his grandmother, and the grandmother said he must leave, so he was living in various places, including sometimes with his father. His father was living with someone else, and also had a drink and drug problem. The Conference was called to discuss the young person's needs, particularly as his unsettled lifestyle meant that he was missing out on school, and there was a likelihood of him becoming 'looked after'.

Attending were the young person, his father, maternal grandmother, paternal grandmother, and a family friend who turned up unexpectedly but was welcomed by the family. The mother decided not to attend, apparently on religious grounds.

The co-ordinator commented that the Conference was interesting from a number of points of view. It brought the two grandmothers together, which was useful. The family friend very successfully acted as an advocate for the young person, at one point saying 'look, nobody is listening to this young person and to what he's trying to say'. And the young person said that he would like to live with his father on two conditions: that he attend Alcoholics Anonymous, and that he stop smoking drugs. This plan was agreed, and the boy went to live with his father.

Unfortunately the father did not stop drinking or smoking. The boy kept reminding him that he should be sticking to the plan and getting help for it. This resulted in the father threatening to beat him up, so the boy left and returned to his mother, with the support of his grandmothers. The placement with his mother continued to be stable.

Plans for the 'child protection' group of children, numbering 35, were implemented successfully except for two children who returned to live at home for a short time before being looked after again (Case 5). In one further child protection case involving two children the family plan was not carried out at all, apparently due to the reluctance of the social workers to implement it.

## Case 5

This Conference concerned a 3 month old baby who had been taken into care following a non-accidental injury. A child protection conference was held and her name was placed on the at-risk register. The child protection conference recommended that a Family Group Conference be held to consider ways of supporting the parents in the care of their child.

The Conference was held in a church hall one weekday day-time, and lasted one and a half hours, most of which was spent by the family alone. Attending were the mother and father, paternal grandfather, paternal grandmother and her partner, paternal great aunt, maternal grandmother, maternal step-grandfather, maternal grandfather and a paternal aunt and uncle. The health visitor and the foster mother joined the social worker as information givers.

The family all felt that the first priority was for the parents to 'sort themselves out', and, in particular, to continue with the counselling they were having. The parents did not want the family to make specific arrangements to care for the baby for them, as they wanted to look after her themselves. It was agreed that the maternal grandmother would care for the child if the mother got a part time job. Some specific suggestions were made for the family to take the mother out socially, and for the mother to join a mother and toddler group.

A second Conference was requested and held one evening just before the baby was to return home. Most of the same family members attended, eight in all, and they all reiterated the fact that 'help is always there if needed'. The parents were again reluctant to be tied down to specific arrangements, but said they would have no hesitation in contacting relatives if they needed help.

Shortly after being reunited with her parents, the baby, by then 6 months old, suffered a further non accidental injury and was removed from the home on a permanent basis.

The majority of the children being looked after at the time of the Family Group Conference for reasons other than child protection also had their plans carried out successfully over the time scale of the follow up. Plans here were more likely to include gradual change, with increasing contact leading to reunion with the family. In two cases, we know that the increased contact was taking place, including with previously out-of-contact parents, but not whether the planned reunion was implemented successfully. In a further case, a young person about to leave care was planning to obtain independent accommodation with family support and this was still being actioned at follow up.

For the three groups of children considered above, placement was a possible issue on the Conference agenda and therefore stability of placement an aspect of 'success'. There was a fourth (small) group of children for whom placement was not at issue, but who were 'in need'. Examples of these were children with parent(s) with a learning disability or who were chronically ill. In these cases a support or care package was needed, and the meeting held for the family to agree the co-ordination and components of care (see Case 6). The information we have from follow up suggests that these plans were very successful in meeting the needs of the child and parents, in reducing replication of services and in avoiding service 'overload' on the family.

## Case 6

In this single parent family the mother had learning difficulties and there were three children in the house, two girls aged 13 and 11, and a boy of 8. The Conference was held in respect of the 8 year old boy, also with learning difficulties, whose behaviour was proving difficult for the mother to manage, and whose educational needs were unclear. The Conference was attended by the children, the mother, maternal grandmother, a maternal great aunt and her husband, and a maternal great uncle. The boy's head teacher attended as an information giver along with representatives of the social services department.

The resulting plan was quite detailed, covering the practical needs of the family, and was written up in the language of the family. The co-ordinator, social worker and head teacher all commented on the positive outcomes of the process:

- The social worker learnt that the mother's aunt had been helping the family with their financial management, and so could arrange to liaise with her once a month.
- The head teacher was able to understand the difficulties the family were in and appreciate their strengths as well as their needs.
- One of the older girls was able to speak up at the Conference to express her sense of responsibility for the family, and her need for support.
- The family were able to use the Conference productively, despite their learning difficulties, and were very pleased to be able to express themselves in their own words.

The plan continued to work for over a year until the family became less able to cope when the mother developed a brain tumour. This change in the situation obviously required further planning and does not detract from the success of the process.

## Did the plans sufficiently protect the children?

Concerns about the Family Group Conference model often centre on the apparent contradiction of asking families to make plans to keep children safe where family members themselves have been involved in neglectful or abusive behaviours. We were therefore particularly interested to know how well protected the children were by the plans made. We have considered this from several different angles: social worker views, rates of registration and deregistration, and re-abuse rates.

### Social workers' views

Social workers for the 'child protection' group of children were asked how well they thought the child had been protected as a result of the Family Group Conference (Table 8.6). The social workers asked thought that two thirds of the children had been better protected, and none felt children had been less well protected as a result of the Family Group Conference. It seems that the social workers are confident that the family groups did implement plans that protected their children. An example of a child being better protected by the involvement of the wider family through the Conference plan is given in Case 7.

**Table 8.6** Social worker views on how well children were protected by Family Group Conference plans.

|  | (% of children) |
| --- | --- |
| Better than they would have been | 67 |
| As well as they would have been | 33 |
| Worse than they would have been | 0 |

## Case 7

Two children, a girl of 1 and a boy of 14 years, were placed on the at-risk register at a child protection conference for reasons of neglect. The mother's drinking problem meant that she was not always able to judge whether she was in a fit state to care for the children and there had been concerns about the safety of the baby and the emotional effect on the boy.

Attending were the mother, the two children, the children's two older sisters and an aunt. The mother would not give any information about the children's fathers, so they could not be contacted; her current boyfriend was invited but did not attend. The meeting lasted over 5 hours, with the family meeting alone for most of that time.

The mother came to the meeting (which started in the morning) the worse for wear for drink. She appeared very agitated and was *acting up.* The co-ordinator had to be active to keep her in the building, which was reported to be very stressful, and at one point the mother left the building and the co-ordinator had to go and look for her.

Despite this the family wrote up their own comprehensive plan with 26 points. The main points relating to the children were that: the aunt would provide alternative care for the baby, if this was necessary; the relatives would check on the household frequently; and the older boy would contact the family if he felt things were out of control. They agreed that 'if after every effort has been made to contact one of the family members with no success it would be acceptable for social services to take the baby temporarily until one of the family can take her'. It was also agreed that the boy could stay with any family members who lived within commuting distance of his school and that he would be positively encouraged to attend school.

Relating to the mother, the family were all committed to supporting the mother on her road to rehabilitation. The family asked for help to rehouse the mother nearer other family members, provide mother with a washing machine, continue the child-minding service and to assist mother with travel expenses to rehabilitation agencies. The mother also asked for help in getting an eviction order against her current boyfriend.

The family wrote that 'we believe it is very important that social services remain involved at this stage. If we feel unable to cope or the situation is out of control, we will ask social services for advice/ assistance'.

The co-ordinator commented that 'that evening the entire family went round to her house and asked the boyfriend to leave, and that's how they got rid of him'. The following weekend a family member found the mother drunk caring for the children so the family plan was put into action. On the Monday the family informed the social services that the aunt was now caring for the children, and were asked if they wanted legal back up. The family initially declined but then requested an interim care order as the mother was trying to undermine the situation. The social services department supported proceedings to grant a residence order to the aunt, until the mother solved her drinking problem. At follow up a year later, the children were still living with the aunt.

### Child protection register data

We looked at the more objective evidence of risk provided by the at-risk register. Whilst this may be an imperfect measure, it is the only nationally available measure of concern regarding child protection. As noted earlier (Table 4.3), a similar proportion of our sample was registered at the time of the Family Group Conference as was found to be registered post child protection conference by Thoburn and her colleagues in their study.

At follow up over half of the children registered at the time of the Conference had been deregistered, leaving 43% of children remaining on the register. This compares favourably with the 82% found to be still on the register at 6 months post child protection conference (Thoburn *et al.*, 1995: p. 120). No children in our study had been placed on the register anew or reregistered up to one year after the Family Group Conference. The figures support the view that the children were comparatively well protected by the plans made, and that there was no increase in child protection concerns post Family Group Conference.

In one case at least (Case 8), the Family Group Conference led to the increased protection of other children, as well as the focus child.

*Re-abuse rates*

A number of studies have looked at the incidence of re-abuse of children after they have been brought to the attention of the social services, often finding rates of between a quarter and a third (see Department of Health, 1995a: pp. 42–43). In a follow up of 304 children attending a child abuse inpatient assessment unit, Levy *et al.* (1995) found a re-abuse rate of 16.8%, with the greatest risk being in the first two years after discharge. Our follow up found that two of the 35 children were re-abused, one (outlined in Case 5 above) suffering non accidental injury, and the other a repeat rejection in a case of emotional abuse, both shortly after the Conference. This puts re-abuse rates in our sample at 6%, considerably lower than other studies would lead us to expect.

## Case 8

> This family consisted of a single mother with two children, a girl of 14 and a boy of 9. There had in the past been a child protection investigation in respect of the girl's allegation of sexual impropriety by her father, which was not conclusive, and a further investigation in respect of the boy's allegation of sexual misconduct by a lodger, also inconclusive.
>
> There had been a breakdown in the relationship between mother and daughter, resulting in the daughter going to stay at a neighbour's and refusing to move. The situation deteriorated when the police were called to intervene in the argument that ensued between mother and the neighbour. Mother was requesting that the daughter be accommodated.
>
> Attending the Conference were mother, father, child, younger brother, father's partner, girl's teacher and four social workers representing different teams. The agreement reached was as follows:

- The child would remain at the neighbour's for 6 weeks.
- The neighbour would be assessed by the resources team as a potential carer.
- A social worker would spend further time with the child trying to re-engage on the sexual abuse issues.
- Father's offer to care for the child would be considered by his local team (he lived about 80 miles away). The girl's stated wish was to live with him.

Shortly after the meeting the mother and child were reconciled, and some family work was offered to help the family. Mother also asked for counselling regarding her own abuse as a child. Father's partner spoke to the girl about her allegations of sexual abuse, questioned her own children and called the police. He is now serving a 5 year sentence for sexual assault on her children.

## Comparing outcomes

We have seen that the overall intent of the plans made was generally carried out and maintained, and that the families and professionals were on the whole satisfied with the implementation. In this section we compare the outcomes with 'what might have been' and with findings from other studies.

### *What would have happened if there had not been a Family Group Conference?*

We put a hypothetical question to social workers: what do you think would have happened if there had not been a Family Group Conference? (We also asked the same question of the co-ordinators, and found their answers to be similar but more likely to be based on actions. For instance, where a social worker said 'the situation would have deteriorated' the co-ordinator took this one step further and said 'the child would have ended up being looked after'.) Clearly, the 'what if' question does not give us definitive answers, but does give us some idea as to possible alternative outcomes for these particular children. Social workers were able to give us their opinion relating to 64 children, two thirds of those in this study, and their views are outlined in Table 8.7.

We can see from Table 8.7 that for almost half of the children the overall outcome was thought to have been the same as it would have been with no Conference, but that the Conference conferred additional benefits in terms of increased family involvement and support. It was also thought that one fifth of the children would probably or definitely have become, or remained 'looked after'. The ages of these 13 children ranged from 3 to 16 years, with an average of 10. For a further group of six children the alternative outcome of becoming or remaining looked

**Table 8.7** Outcomes of Family Group Conferences compared with social workers' views of what might have happened.

| If no FGC, outcome predicted by social worker | % (of children) |
|---|---|
| Same outcome but less distress/more speedy resolution | 8 |
| Same outcome | 14 |
| Same outcome but less family or other support | 48 |
| Worse outcome: possibly looked after | 9 |
| Worse outcome: probably/definitely looked after (or remaining looked after) | 20 |

after was thought to be a 'possibility' and for 26 of the 'same' children there was an acknowledged risk of entry into care. The latter would seem to be in another category: an 'unlikely but possibly looked after' group. Although these are only estimates of what might have happened, it seems very likely that some children were kept out of the care system by the use of the Family Group Conference.

Alongside the outcomes above, there were also benefits (and savings) relating to other parts of the child care system. It was estimated that at least seven children avoided further child protection procedures and/or court proceedings by being involved in the Family Group Conference process. (An example is given in Case 9.) There were also the advantages for all associated with early deregistration, and the increased protection of children.

## Case 9

The central issue of this case concerning a 7 year old girl was that the child had described serious sexual abuse by her father, who was now separated from the mother. The allegation was absolutely credited by the social worker, guardian *ad litem* and the consultant psychiatrist brought in to give an opinion on the videoed memorandum interview, but the child had retracted her allegations in the face of her family's reaction and social services were unsure who, if anyone, in the family could adequately protect her from recurrence. The social services department had obtained an interim care order following the investigation, and were applying for a full care order. Five family members were separately applying for residence orders and a 5 day court hearing was scheduled for a month following the Family Group Conference. The Conference was convened to ensure family members were aware of the reasons for concern and to establish common ground for planning for the child's future care.

Attending were the mother, father, paternal grandmother, maternal grandfather, maternal step-grandmother, and father's ex-partner. The child did not wish to attend. In addition to the family and the social worker, the guardian *ad litem* attended, with the confidentiality of his role made explicit and accepted by the family.

The family agreed to support the social services application for a full care order, with the child to be placed with her previous carer, the father's ex-partner, with the request that she be assessed and supported formally as a foster carer. The father was planning to obtain work abroad within the next 2 months, which would remove him from concern. The plan also stated that if the foster carer assessment and the father's move abroad could not be accomplished, the child should be placed with foster carers outside the family, with regular contact with family members.

Agreement was reached on the plan and the applications for residence orders were withdrawn, thus avoiding the contested hearing. A full care order was obtained and the child was eventually placed in a long term adoption placement with the parents' cooperation.

The clear message from the social workers was that for the majority of the children the plans made at Family Group Conferences led to better outcomes for the children.

## Did the plans cost less or more than expected?

We can now compare the rough overall costs of the plans with the costs of 'what might have happened'. This will give us some information on the relative costs and savings of the plans made. Again, we are aware that in the absence of detailed costings of services requested and of those previously provided or potentially available we can only present an estimated view of the situation based on placements. However, major costs are those involved with the funding of placements and not the funding of fieldwork time, so some work can be done to provide a crude but indicative summary on the basis of the extremes of costs, using placement provision as a high cost example, and increases in social worker time costs or one-off payments as a low cost example.

The plans were categorised into those more, less or equally costly overall than the outcomes predicted without the Family Group Conference, and the information on 69 plans is given in Table 8.8. The majority of plans cost less (55%) or the same (39%) as expected. Only 6% cost more overall, all of them high cost plans: in two of these family requests for specialist residential treatment placements were agreed and in both cases costs were shared between agencies. In two other cases the higher costs were due to the child continuing in residential care but additional funding being agreed for extra support or contact. Overall

**Table 8.8** Relative costs of Family Group Conference plans compared with costs of other predicted outcomes.

|  |  | More (%) | Less (%) | Equal (%) |
|---|---|---|---|---|
| High | (*n* = 17) | 6 | 3 | 16 |
| Medium | (*n* = 31) | 0 | 30 | 14 |
| Low | (*n* = 21) | 0 | 22 | 9 |

*n* = number of plans

there is no evidence that the plans were expensive, compared to what might have been expected for these children.

## Placement outcomes: comparison with other studies

Looking further at what could have been expected to happen if there had not been a Family Group Conference, we have compared our outcomes at follow up with those obtained in other studies.

### 'Looked after' children

We used information from the study by Bullock and his colleagues (1993) on placement outcomes for a group of 31 looked after children as a source of possible comparison with our sample of 35 looked after children (Table 8.9). The comparison should be treated with caution as the two groups were not selected on identical criteria: their group was of children who were expected to return home, whilst ours was of those who were referred for a Family Group Conference because plans were needed. It should also be noted that follow up time is different in the two studies, but we think that in our study the possibility of some home placements breaking down in the next 6 months is probably balanced

**Table 8.9** Placement outcomes for looked after children with and without Family Group Conference.

|  | FGC (follow up 12 months) (%) | Bullock et al. (1993) (follow up 18 months) (%) |
|---|---|---|
| All returners | 62 | 64 |
| Returned and stayed home | 56 | 29 |
| Returned but moved on | 6 | 35 |
| Remained in care | 38 | 35 |

by the possibility that some remaining looked after children would return home.

The data strongly suggest that our 'looked after and in need of plans' sample had the same proportion of children returning home as the 'looked after and expected to return home' sample, but that our returners were more likely to remain at home rather than move on to another placement. There is sufficient difference to suggest that the Family Group Conference is likely to have contributed to the increased stability of the placement over time.

Bullock and his colleagues also used new data from their 'lost in care' study to look at the composition of the household that the children were returning to. Their data concern 269 returners and we have compared it to our sample of 24 returners (Table 8.10). The sample sizes and populations are again different, and the figures from the comparative study have within them a number of temporary placements that were always intended to return home, which will substantially reduce the percentage going to parents. Nonetheless the figures are very different: for 40% of the our looked after group returning home from care, *home* was wholly or partly with wider family members. It appears that the Family Group Conference is likely to provide at least some increase in the use of relatives to provide care.

**Table 8.10** Placements of children returning from care, with and without Family Group Conference.

|  | FGC (%) | Bullock et al. *(1993)* (%) |
| --- | --- | --- |
| To natural parent(s) | 60 | 94 |
| To relatives | 36 | 6 |
| Parent/relative shared care | 4 | 0 |

We cannot automatically infer from the above findings – that placements are more stable and that more placements are with *relatives* – that placements with relatives are more stable. There may be other factors relating to the process of the Family Group Conference, such as the agreement and support of the family group to the plan, that confer stability on placements of whichever kind.

### Child protection cases

We also compared the placement pattern of our group of child protection children 6 months after Family Group Conference to that of 219 children 6 months after child protection conference (Thoburn *et al.*, 1995: p. 81). We again found that the proportion of children remaining looked after is very similar but that the wider family is more likely to be involved in providing placements for children.

## Unplanned outcomes

We have already seen from Chapter 6 that families are on the whole positive about using the model, and that social workers who have used it are often enthusiastic. Here we are interested in the effects of the process on the participants generally. Are there genuine spin-off benefits, and if so for whom, and in what way?

### Families

Family members themselves commented on the *side effects* of the meeting. Barker and Barker (1995: p. 12) found some members of each family reporting changes that had occurred such as 'more open discussion, new learning about the dynamics of family relationships and seeing the issue from a new perspective'. They also reported that in six of the seven Conferences they studied, family members met together who had not spoken to each other for some considerable time, either because of family rows or geographical distance.

Lupton and her colleagues asked family members whether 'participating in the Family Group Conference had any effect on your relationships with other members of the family?' and found 16% agreed that it had, but some of these reported negative effects such as decreased contact with the child, rather than positive spin-offs. We are not sure whether the differences in these findings reflect the different interview schedules or the different types of families being referred to the projects early on in their history.

However, as we saw in Chapter 6, both the Lupton and the Barker and Barker studies quote family members reflecting on their own experiences of family difficulties, and seeing the Family Group Conference as a positive way of improving things and 'getting things out in the open'. The process is seen as beneficial by many family members whether the plan is successful or not. In addition, a number of families were reported to have resolved to 'get together' again to sort out any future problems, indicating a learning process relating to problem solving.

Social workers also very often made comments regarding their perception of the effects of the meetings on family functioning. They specifically mentioned improvements in family relationships and family understanding of the situation in a third of the families involved. Even in cases where the plans were not carried out fully social workers talked about how the experience of the meeting and of 'trying' had improved interfamily relationships and 'enabled bridges to be built within the family network'. They estimated that in about two thirds of cases, distant or out-of-contact family members had become more involved with the child and the family through the process. Social workers also gave examples of how the Conference had enabled other needs to be recognised, for instance children were able to speak up for their own needs (see also Case 6).

## Social workers

We asked social workers whether they thought that their experience of the project, either directly or through the team involvement, had resulted in any knock on effect on their work. The answers from 62 social workers can be divided into three groups. Almost half fell into a 'positive benefits' group, saying that the model had made them think more positively about families and improved their partnership practice:

> 'You can't help but view people differently, you can't help but give people more decision making powers in their lives even when there isn't a Family Group Conference because you soak in the ethos of Family Group Conferences.'

A smaller group of around a fifth of social workers said that the model had confirmed their ideas and provided a framework for their partnership practice, rather than actually changing their practice. A number of these talked about the model helping them to 'remember things they already knew'. The third, 'no effect' group saw the model as 'just another way of working' that had done nothing for them.

When we considered their replies in the light of their experience of Family Group Conferences, we found that those who had engaged in the project by referring families for a Conference were significantly more likely to report changes in their partnership practice. Their subsequent attendance at a meeting was not significant. This suggests that it was their engagement with the principles of the model which affected their practice *and* led them to refer to the project, rather than it being the evidence of the outcomes of the meeting which led to changes.

## Families and social workers

Neither our interviews nor those in other studies asked questions directly relating to the relationship between the family and the social services or other agencies. However there are strong indications that the relationship was affected. For instance, some social workers spoke of 'more open working' and 'communication barriers being broken down'. Family members commented on everyone being 'on a par', no 'them and us'. Co-ordinators reported family members 'growing in confidence', feeling more 'in control of how they work with social services rather than the other way round'. All of these, together with the consensus of professional views that the model has the potential to empower families, suggest that the model does have a positive impact on partnership between families and professionals. We are hoping to have the opportunity to explore this aspect of the Family Group Conference model in future research.

## Conclusions

The Family Group Conference process nearly always results in agreed, workable plans. The expectations the plans place on agency resources may not differ greatly from plans made through other processes, although the range and nature of services requested may differ. However, family resources feature highly in family plans, often in creative ways, including family members offering to care for children. The plans are implemented at a rate comparable to those made elsewhere, and the overall intent of the plans is carried out in a high percentage of cases.

Outcomes for the children are positive in that placements appear to be stable and contact with the wider family is increased. Indicators such as registration on the at-risk register, re-abuse rates and estimates of 'what might have been' all suggest that the plans both protect and benefit the children. They also appear to reduce demands on expensive service costs such as state care, court procedures and child protection processes. Experience of the Family Group Conference model can also have a broader positive effect on the family members and social workers involved, increasing understanding of what are often very complex situations, and improving problem solving skills through partnership practice.

# Chapter 9

# The Next Stages

It is evident from the research reported in the previous chapters that Family Group Conferences have many positive contributions to make to child welfare services. This chapter reviews some of those contributions, and outlines key issues that will need to be borne in mind when moving on to the next stage of developing this work.

## Child welfare, partnership and Family Group Conferences

In the first three chapters of this book we outlined the case, now a central part of the Children Act 1989, for social services and families working in partnership in order to improve children's welfare. Much of what the family does, even when in contact with social services, could be seen as child welfare work. Indeed the judgements being made about the seriousness of particular problems, the need to get the involvement of key players and the aim of gaining the maximum practical commitment to change could all be seen as part and parcel of much of family life, as well as some of the key tasks undertaken by child welfare professionals.

Clearly some families fail to do some or all of the relevant child welfare tasks, but in many of the circumstances it is not families that are failing but households: a carer or young person, or an external family member, will often be the one that needs to change their behaviour. It will on occasions be more than one person, but very rarely indeed is it going to be whole extended families who are failing children. Even at the extreme end of child welfare problems, where children are abused, it looks likely that wider involvement will often be possible, and may well pay dividends. As one summary of research has recently pointed out: 'the portrayal of the social isolation of maltreating families from research studies is breathtakingly shallow, with little evidence for the comprehensive insularity commonly believed to be true of them' (Thompson, 1995). Families, despite the lack of attention paid to them, extend beyond the household. *Family* and *household* often mean the same thing in conversation, and they nearly always mean the same thing in statistics and newspaper articles, but in everyday life, even poor quality everyday life, family is usually much more than this.

The extended family still has a prominent role in modern Britain, but a largely unsung one. Within the social science literature the practical role of extended family and the psychological contribution of family, of *roots*, is once again being explored, but we should remember it has always been the living reality for children and families despite its low profile in professional debate! As we discussed in earlier chapters, social services have in general been rather poor at recognising this reality. It is important to make sure that partnership extends beyond households to include the psychological and practical value of wider family.

It was in this context that the introduction of Family Group Conferences in the mid 1990s seemed particularly timely. They seemed to provide a practical and innovative way of developing some of the ideals of partnership and they did so in a manner which reflected the importance of the family in the upbringing of children. The way that they were fitted within a legal frame provided another reason to experiment with them, as they also seemed to provide some answers to the way that the law must balance the needs of children against over-intrusive invasions into people's lives. Within youth justice they provided another interesting element, as the central role of the victim brought a much neglected player back into the actions of the justice system.

There were sound reasons to experiment with these new ideas, and the results of that experiment, as laid out in the previous chapters, have been positive. It seems very likely that Family Group Conferences will have a part to play in generating better partnership between users and staff in child welfare, and in making a small contribution to developing a greater sense of 'family and community integrity' (Hassall, 1996: p. 34). This is very important. Modern pressures, whether of work or lack of it, whether of suburban housing with its attendant journeys, or poor city housing with little available transport, seem to push people into increasingly private compartments, albeit with ways to communicate from within them, such as the telephone, that help to maintain contact beyond them. There is always the threat that human contact will diminish, and interaction reduce, in the rush of modern problems that face us around the turn of the century. Making sure that family and community life is reasonably vibrant, and certainly does not degrade, is important to us all: the regeneration of family and community life may become an important agenda item over the coming years.

Family and community life is important to us all, and this certainly includes those who come into contact with the social services. Family Group Conferences represent an attempt to provide a certain regeneration of family and community problem solving in this context. They bring cooperation and mutual support to the centre of the stage, alongside a genuine respect for the importance of family within children's and adults' lives. In order to achieve these aims, welfare services need a high standard of practice based on cooperation and respect, and which provides, for example, good clear information, and in an open and honest manner. It needs to be a service that respects, and supports, different cultures, religions, languages, and heritage.

Decent, good, respectful work is the foundation on which Family Group Conferences can develop. Their particular contribution, which requires this foundation, consists of four elements which we have explored at various stages in the book:

- The independent co-ordinator role
- The wide understanding of the meaning of *family*
- The careful use of private family time as part of the decision-making process
- The deliberate attempt to negotiate agreement between all the relevant parties

These elements make a difference. The experience of Conferences, as we have described, is not the same as the experience of other meetings. We have found various ways to put this in the course of the book, but perhaps the last word on this difference is best left to a mother who, in relatively quick succession, experienced the *standard* system and the Conference one. Her story is given below.

## A case history, as told by a mother

### Background

The parents of a 7 year old boy (we will call him Alan) and his older brother had split up, with the older boy going to live with his father, who subsequently remarried, and Alan living with his mother. Alan's mother recounted the stresses she and her son were under, 'doing 14 or 16 hour days keeping body and soul together', experiencing difficulties with contact visits to Alan's father and brother due to acrimony between the adults and living in temporary accommodation. Alan's behaviour deteriorated both at home and at school to such an extent that the mother ended up *snapping* and hitting him, then taking him to the police station asking for help. He was fostered and placed on the at risk register. He and his mother were offered counselling, and the mother tried to sort out her housing difficulties. Nine months later, after several attempts, which were abandoned due to organisational problems, there was a child protection conference to consider whether Alan should be deregistered. By this time the local authority was suggesting that the foster placement should be permanent if the mother could not take him back. The mother still did not have suitable accommodation, and felt very frustrated that 'nobody was really looking at how Alan needed to see his brother, and we needed to have our own place'. She decided to move Alan from foster care to family care, at her sister's, until she could complete arrangements for accommodation. The sister happened to live in an area where there was a Family Group Conference project. A month after he moved a Family Group Conference was organised with Alan, Alan's mother, the mother's new partner, Alan's father and the father's new wife to sort out plans for the boy.

The mother described the two different meetings to us:

### The child protection conference

The mother said she hadn't had any choice about where this conference should be held. She knew something about the system from some of the work she had done in the past, but if she hadn't had that basic knowledge:

> 'it would've been pretty frightening, pretty frightening for anybody because you have a police person, social services solicitor, a social worker, we had the foster parent, we had the foster parent's supervisor who I'd never met before, we had a chairperson who comes from somewhere else and I'd never met them, we had a health worker ... I mean here we had at least eight people in the room, we only knew two.

> These conferences that you have to have, whether it's child protection or just even a general meeting with your social worker, foster parent or whatever – something goes wrong basically, something somewhere goes wrong. You've got no control at all, none, there isn't any. And it's your life, it's your child ... in the end you get so despondent'.

### The Family Group Conference

> 'Alan was allowed to participate as well ... and this isn't just for the one "family" ... if you've got grandparents that want to speak up and voice an opinion they've got a right if that's what they wanted to do. She [the co-ordinator] was really good because she did all the running around informing everybody, defining what it was going to be for, the questions to be raised.

> The co-ordinator suggested they had a place to hold it, with a garden, French doors leading onto a garden – if children get bored or adults get excited the child can disappear slowly out of the door and not be affected and come in and be free to come and go. Same for adults if you get aerated just get up, go for a walk, come back, sit down. And they laid on sandwiches, tea, there was toys for the children. If you didn't want to use that or you wanted something with a bit more of a regime instead of a relaxed atmosphere then they would've offered a room. We were phoned with possible dates, it was all agreed.

The social worker was there to offer and give information about the services that were available, and help if there was any immediate problems to be resolved. The co-ordinator said "Well I'll leave you to it but if you get stuck or there's something you want to know or it gets out of hand, call me back in again". More like a referee would really. Alan was allowed to say what he wanted and basically we said "what do you want to do?" and all he said was "I want to see my brother". And once his dad heard this he just said "well then..." ...I think a lot of it really is breaking the ice. If you haven't spoken to somebody for like a few years. If you can get over that barrier and just sort of stick to what you're supposed to be sticking to, then it can be quite good.

We had as much time as we liked. I think we got there something like one o'clock. And it was pointed out again if we couldn't come to agreement on that particular day, no problem, let's see how far we've got, I'm sure we would have gone down and analysed how far we had got. And then reset another meeting. And keep resetting until you can come to an agreement.

We still don't have a lot to do with his father's side of the family. We speak because we have to speak. It's been a year, it's been reasonably successful. Now we've got it to a stage where if I've got to go on holiday or the dad's going on holiday or Alan's not well, now I will pick up the phone and I'll say "well sorry, he can't come because he's got chicken pox" or whatever. I'd say for a good four years, we'd pass each other on the street. I mean literally pass each other on the street and not even smile.

If it hadn't worked out quite honestly I think that we would have had to go back to a family conference and I would have had to put it all on the table and say look, you know you're confusing him. But now we can say "You're the child, we're adults, we are going to phone each other to sort things out".

## On the model in general

'It's different, because you are in control. I'm not that incapable that I can't say things for myself. So somebody may translate what I say in a different way, they'll get it wrong, and then they've actually not really said what I said in the beginning. So you're better off wherever you've got an opportunity speaking for yourself. And you don't even have to be reasonably educated, you just turn round and say I don't want that, I don't like that.

The family conference co-ordinator is there to speak to the second party on your behalf. And it's a well known fact that a lot of people are hostile towards social workers, so I think it helps if it's not a social worker or it doesn't come under that banner. It's not as frightening for people and they're willing and more prepared to let that person in their home and listen, at least listen to what they've got to say.

It was more friendly, you can ask any question you like. I think in general the family case conference, they save you going through law courts, because that can be a humiliating experience as well. That's just solicitors, again you're not allowed to actually voice your own opinion, you've got this person speaking gobbledygook for somebody else that doesn't know them. Being slandered and libelled all over the place by your ex-partner, and you're not really in control. You can contest it and you can say "excuse me" and stop the proceedings. But then it just drags on, it just drags on and on and on. It's worse, it's just not healthy. And no break-up is ever going to be amicable, never going to be. But a lot of it is where you're in control all the time, even if you're rowing together in your own home you're in control. The minute you've got outside bodies involved you are no longer in control.

It's like some of the other conferences and meetings that you go to, they're so formal that you can actually feel initially intimidated. It is, it's like going to court. You feel intimidated, you're intimidated. And so an area where you can take away the intimidation and allow people to feel reasonably less restricted, it's a lot better. You can actually talk to people instead of screaming and shouting at each other, you can actually talk to each other. You'd be surprised probably, a lot of people if they took the plunge would probably be surprised that the person that they once lived lived with, instead of screaming at, because the last few years practically all they've done is scream at each other, can actually now communicate. And they're communicating over a common denominator, it's a common denominator and it's the child. The child is what keeps your feet on the ground rather than up in the air. Because when you're living together and you're arguing about each other, kids get forgotten because you're having a go at each other. But if you're in a room and your one sole reason for being there is that one common denominator that keeps bringing you back together, then it's best to sort out the arrangements. If you don't want to see that much of each other anyway, then sort out the arrangements. I think there'd be a lot of people out there who'd be quite frightened. For one reason or another. The fact they've had a violent partner, perhaps they're so easily intimidated, because they are very timid, a lot of people after a course of going through the various systems, their confidence is like below zero. Then I think then yes, those people would need confidence building first. They'd need to be helped. I don't mean psychiatrically counselled, I mean helped in positive ways to rebuild their self-confidence, to enable them to take charge of their own thoughts and well-being.

There comes a time when you think "I can take control now", and that's when I think the normal way of running social services departments falls down. Yes people come initially because they do need a certain amount of support and a certain amount of help. But if you go on trying and nursemaid and suffocate that person then their growth isn't going to take place. The social services, the way it's run at the moment actually doesn't allow the person who has to to take control, they're very reluctant to give that person back the control of the family. So social services becomes the head of the family, and the mother and the father, or one of them, becomes more or less like a child themselves, and they regress into no responsibility, because they're instructed all the way, what their responsibilities are. But they are not actually helped to rebuild their confidence to enable them to take up the full responsibility.

I think even a woman that has really reached the lowest ebb, given enough support, counselling and guidance, I think eventually, even if it took 20 meetings, as long as she can see that she's taking an important role in the decision-making, then she will eventually come off social services' list altogether. So totally different structure altogether. I think it's probably the best invention that anybody's had.'

## Costs and benefits

An overall appraisal of Family Group Conferences requires some consideration of the relative costs and benefits of the model, to both the participants and to the funding agencies. There are, of course, difficulties in trying to draw up a *balance sheet*, because of the different levels of interest represented, from the individual child concerned to the tax payer contributing to the social services budget. We are also hampered, as we have already said, by the lack of detailed information on service costs relating to most parts of the child care system. Despite this, we think it worthwhile to attempt this exercise, first by reviewing the beneficial outcomes we have identified and considering whether these have resulted in savings to the state, and then evaluating the level of overall costs involved in running Family Group Conferences, both financial and otherwise.

### Outcomes

The study of 80 Family Group Conferences shows that the model can be used successfully in all areas of child welfare. The families involved were no *easier* to work with, and the children no different, from others to be found on a social worker's case load. Indeed, there is some indication that the model tended to be used with more difficult cases, where workers were *stuck* or where relationships between the family and the statutory services were poor. Certainly anxieties were high amongst social workers that families would not manage to meet because of interpersonal disputes, and if they did meet there could be serious, possibly violent, consequences. These anxieties were unfounded: family members did attend, listen, discuss and produce acceptable, often creative plans.

On the *plus* side of the balance sheet we therefore have the success of the model in resulting in agreed plans, of the 80 conferences, 74 rendered full agreement. It could be considered a positive that the plans included reasonable requests for help from social services, often in conjunction with educational and health services. Families took the concerns seriously, and acknowledged the needs of the situation. They did not seek to avoid agency involvement, but neither were they greedy for agency resources. Plans nearly always included elements of family help and support, which conferred a number of benefits on the child, the main carers and the agencies working with the family.

The research shows not only the families' willingness to contribute to the well-being of their children, but their success in providing children with a safe and individual 'place in the world'. Children are more likely to be living with members of the wider family, placements are more likely to be stable and children appear to be rather better protected than would be expected following decisions made through other processes. These all point to the model as one contributing to the strengthening of links within families.

Although many participants found the Conferences demanding and difficult, they also recognised the benefits of 'meeting together to sort things out', of 'getting things out in the open' and of 'understanding what was going on better'. The process itself was therefore satisfactory to the great majority of the family members and the professionals, a positive finding in relation to creating a way of working together. Social workers tend to approve of the model in theory, at least in public, but about a third do not refer cases, finding some difficulties with the sharing responsibility and power that is involved. Those who do engage with the model, however, are often relieved to share their concerns and responsibilities with the family. They also tend to report a knock-on effect on the rest of their work: if you can imagine genuinely working in partnership in one part of your work, you cannot easily continue in your *old ways* in the rest of your work.

Social work generally could benefit greatly from the Family Group Conference model. Previously reluctant families may be positively engaged, and views of practitioners and services improved. Such changes have been reported elsewhere, for instance Boffa (1995) reports the creation of a more positive view of social services in Melbourne. The model also provides the opportunity for social workers to work in partnership, and perhaps to move from 'theory espoused' to 'theory in action' (Argyris & Schön, 1978).

## Possible savings

What are the financial implications of our findings? As we saw in Chapter 8, there was no indication that the plans were any more expensive to implement overall, and many were thought to have been less expensive than they would otherwise have been. More specifically, it was estimated by social workers that 13 children would probably or definitely have needed state care, with its associated costs, if the family had not been involved in planning through the Family Group Conference. Using this 'probable or definite' group of children, aged 10 on average, we can suggest estimates of savings made. For instance, if each had been 'looked after' for 1 year there would have been 13 care years saved, or if each had been 'looked after' for 2 years there would have been 26 care years saved.

We could also consider the six children who 'possibly' would have needed state care, and the 26 for whom it was a risk, but not really expected. To make an estimate of savings from these groups would be even more of a shot in the dark than the above suggestions, but we do not think the potential savings from this group should be ignored entirely. In the absence of data on the effect of large-scale introduction of the Family Group Conference model on the population of 'looked after' children in the UK, the outcome in this respect has to remain a matter of conjecture.

However, in addition to the 'probable' or 'possible' savings in state care, we are confident in pointing to savings relating to:

- Reduced court costs because plans were agreed
- Fewer child protection conferences because plans adequately protected the children and re-abuse rates were low
- Less intensive resource input needed because of deregistration rates
- Reduction in time and placement costs due to increased stability of placements

We are reluctant to try to quantify these savings, but all the indicators point in the same direction: the model reduces the demand on social service department resources.

### No increases

Despite the tentative nature of these findings, the fact is that each aspect of the model we consider suggests a saving. None of the savings are likely to be massive, although reducing or avoiding even one long-term placement in state care is potentially very significant. Each part of the picture contributes towards the whole, and we therefore feel confident in saying that some resources are saved by the use of this model. Our confidence is perhaps increased by the similarity of our findings to those being reported from around the world. But how do the possible savings compare to the costs?

## Costs

The direct cost of each Family Group Conference results from the cost of the co-ordinator time and expenses, and the costs of the meeting, including for the venue, refreshments and travel. Information from the UK projects suggests each conference costs somewhere in the range of £400 to £800. These costs may be pushed higher by particular circumstances, for instance travel costs for family members living far afield, but most will be at the lower end of this range. The meeting costs reported by Pennell and Burford (1995b) are reassuringly similar. The costs of the introductory work, primarily for training and project management, also need to be considered. Maintenance costs of supervision and on-going training should be comparable to those required from existing work.

It is difficult to say which way a balance tips when the financial costs of running the Conferences are put against the savings resulting from them. A good case could be made for saying that the model produces small savings but, acknowledging the lack of detailed evidence, we prefer to assert that the model is cost neutral.

### Other costs

Although we found many benefits for the child, the family and the professionals, we must consider the costs of the model to the participants. Certainly there are some costs to the family: the process demands a lot of them and sometimes the resulting plans are demanding too. Some families decline the challenge altogether, but those who become involved seem more than willing to bear the costs. Even those for whom the experience is painful or unproductive maintain that the process was worthwhile. We should perhaps be wary of assuming this to be the case, and in this respect it is good to note that direct services to families are continuing at about the present rate.

For the social workers involved, there are the general discomforts and stresses of working with a new model and learning new skills, and the more specific demands on their time each Conference presents, often at a time when the case is in crisis.

### The balance sheet

We can use the above to draw up a very rough balance sheet of the costs and benefits accruing to the main sponsors and participants in the Family Group Conference process (Fig. 9.1).

## Implementation

Despite the positive outcomes, and the likelihood of it being broadly cost neutral to introduce Family Group Conferences, there are a

| COSTS | BENEFITS |
|---|---|
| **Social service departments** | **Social service departments** |
| *Finance* | *Finance* |
| • Setting up the projects | • Care years saved |
| • Conferences at £400–£800 each | • Fewer child protection proceedings |
| | • Avoidance of court costs |
| *Systems* | *Systems* |
| • Implementation difficulties | • More 'working together' |
| | • Improved user/public image |
| **Family/child** | **Family/child** |
| • Process hampered plans for 8% | • Process improved outcomes for 78% |
| • Some families experience more disputes | • Family rifts often healed |
| | • 66% better protected |
| | • Indications of lower re-abuse rate |
| | • Indications of greater deregistration |
| | • Placements more stable |
| | • Contact with wider family increased |
| | • 'Things out in the open' |
| | • Requesting services needed |
| **Social worker** | **Social worker** |
| • Time taken over setting up of conference | • Movement in *stuck* cases |
| • Perceived loss of power | • Clarity of role and responsibility |
| • Initial stress in using a new model | • Improved partnership practice |

**Fig. 9.1** Balancing costs and benefits.

number of reasons to be cautious about their widespread use. They centre around the difficulties of implementation that were found in this project. Two factors stand out in particular, first the need for high quality co-ordinators and second the way in which innovation from individuals and groups has played a role in their success.

## Co-ordinator abilities

The skills of the co-ordinators are central to the working of the Conferences. As we saw in Chapter 5 the major review of the working of the new Act in New Zealand described co-ordinators as the 'linchpin' of Family Group Conferences (Mason *et al.*, 1992: p. 66). Others have made a similar point, for example Boffa's work in Melbourne (1995), and Pennell and Burford (1995b: p. 264) in Canada. There is no question that this role is difficult and requires a combination of perseverance, belief, knowledge and skills that is not everyday. In terms of our theatre metaphor it requires the organising ability of the stage manager, the technical skills of designers and the creativity and verve of directors. There are some outstanding co-ordinators associated with the research we have outlined, but whether they could be recruited in large numbers is at present unknown. Indeed the way they should be selected, trained, supervised and supported still needs a great deal more work.

## Innovation and bureaucratisation

In order to get these projects established, as we have described in earlier chapters, a combination of managers and practitioners worked over, above and around their jobs, they put in hours that they did not have to do, they found imaginative ways around procedural obstacles, they negotiated for long periods and they provided drive and commitment which was often very impressive. At least some work like this may be necessary for the notable success of the projects described. Staff who are on the receiving end of this sort of attention may well perform better. In a famous experiment in a manufacturing company it was found that paying attention to staff had effects on their work independently of the actual changes that were made; productivity went up when lighting was altered one way, and it still went up when the lighting was altered in the opposite way (Roethlisberger & Dickson, 1939). Family Group Conferences do require commitment, they are anything but routine. Recruiting people to take them forward may not be easy, but of course there may be many in social services who would, if given the chance, blossom in a role like this.

Innovatory practice is at the heart of Family Group Conferences, they are by definition tailor-made for each family, and each one is a unique challenge. Practice needs to be imaginative, but underpinned by explicit values. This work requires high quality co-ordinators and energetic supporters. It also requires the right setting and climate. It requires first line managers/supervisors to provide some space for it to flourish in, and preferably to support it (as has been suggested with regard to other changes, see for example: Sinclair *et al.*, 1990; Stevenson & Parsloe, 1993). It is unlikely to flourish in a context of proceduralisation and bureaucratisation of practice, and there are indications that this may be growing within UK social services (Howe, 1992). The experience of New Zealand shows that widespread institutional establishment of the Conferences can work, but it would be sensible to be somewhat cautious as we proceed to future developments, and to be aware of the need to keep genuine agency support high on the agenda, and to make sure that the quality of the Conferences is not undermined by the rules, regulations and underlying philosophy of the agency itself.

## Developing the Conferences

The overall message of this research is that the greater involvement of family, and the greater sharing of power represented in Family Group Conferences, pays good dividends for the welfare of children. Moving ahead with Conferences as one of the options in the child welfare system is clearly worthwhile. Apart from the notes of caution sounded above what else should we pay particular attention to in the next stages of the development? As already discussed we need some more work on the relevant skills, knowledge and attitude combinations for co-ordinators. In addition we must think about the place of the Conferences within child protection procedures (for example should they replace, precede or follow child protection conferences), and other areas for Conference work should be explored (for example adult services, family law, leaving care). Finally, but perhaps most importantly, feedback and research are needed both to guide the endeavours and to keep the spirit of innovation and learning alive in the next phases of the work.

### Feedback and research

There is clearly a need for more research, although it must be borne in mind that the current level of research is probably more than many other new ideas have been subject to, and certainly more than has been carried out on many *established* services. Repeating material on family views, or on basic outcomes, may be useful but of greater value would be the examination of new areas of use, changes in networks, links with other services and the way that Conferences affect family views of social services, and there is much to be said for trying to do more on comparative outcomes for both this work and, equally importantly, for many of the areas of work within child welfare.

Perhaps the most pressing need is to make sure that a research-like stance is built directly into the model itself. Families and professionals need to contribute directly to continuing refinement and development. There could, for example, be an additional stage to the model of the Conference which provides feedback to the parties involved about progress for the child, allowing co-ordinators to learn, families to hold services to account and social services to take risks and develop. This stage, not to be confused with the task of monitoring progress, which will always be needed from either families or social workers or both, could ideally use some brief indicators developed jointly with users and staff. If it was to occur it would echo the spirit of cooperative developmental research, designed to improve outcomes for children, which has been at the basis of the work described in this book.

## The way forward

Attempting to establish partnership-based approaches within social work has not been easy, and Family Group Conferences will be no exception to this. Developing and expanding the work described in this study will involve bright, skilful persistence. Once established there will be a necessity to guard against the possible degradation of the model, as routinisation takes the place of innovation. Over 20 years ago Moroney described this process, the way that services take over new developments and then convert them into inflexible systems. He put it like this:

'For any number of reasons, whether organisational requirements or professional satisfaction, services that were introduced initially as possible mechanisms to assist people with need, quickly became the way to do things. Services that were seen as potentially of benefit became solutions whose benefit is rarely questioned. Innovation is replaced with caution, and flexibility with formal structures.'

(Moroney, 1976: p. 105)

Family Group Conferences require flexibility, within a broad formal frame, they require innovation, and a capacity to recognise that each one is unique and that the strength of the decision-making resides, in part, in this uniqueness. If they are to grow and flourish then the agencies running them will need to nurture this side, and to support the co-ordinators and the project leaders, who will, no doubt, appear at times as troublesome gadflies. When the agency is dealing with the Conferences it will need to tolerate, or better, to support the values that underpin them: to have respect for different views and cultures, to be prepared to listen to all family members, to look for strengths alongside the problems.

A strategy for the implementation of Family Group Conferences will probably work best if it includes a widespread package of family support measures, with developments like Homestart, NEWPIN, and a variety of other family-centred services (see for example the services outlined in Gibbons, 1992). The move to refocus UK social services for children away from an exclusive focus on child protection towards more inclusive family support is a helpful strategy (Association of Directors of Social Services and NCH Action for Children, 1996; Department of Health, 1995a). As we have discussed earlier a strategy like this, that involves Family Group Conferences, must not destroy the Conferences' spirit by too much regulation and guidance. National standards might help, national procedures would be unlikely to do so. In the future there could be mediocre Conferences compulsorily carried out in certain predefined circumstances, or there could be high quality Conferences widely available as one of the options within child welfare services. The mediocre Conference may be better than no Conference at all, but we do not know this. We do know that good Conferences help children and families, and that throughout child welfare work they can be one of 'the best inventions that anyone has had'.

# References

Abrams, M. (1992) A response to the 'Children's Rights approach'. *Family Law Bulletin*, 3(9), 104–109.

Adcock, M., White, R. & Hollows, A. (eds) (1991) *Significant Harm*. Significant Publications, Croydon.

Alder, C. & Wundersitz, J. (eds) (1994) *Family Conferencing and Juvenile Justice – The Way Forward or Misplaced Optimism?* Australian Institute of Criminology, Canberra.

Allan, G. (1996) *Kinship and Friendship in Modern Britain*. Oxford University Press, Oxford.

Allen, R. (1996) *Children and Crime – Taking Responsibility*. Institute for Public Policy Research, London.

Argyris, C. & Schön, D. (1978) *Organisational Learning*. Addison-Wesley, Reading, MA.

Association of Directors of Social Services & NCH Action for Children (1996) *Children Still in Need: Refocusing Child Protection in the Context of Children in Need*. NCH Action for Children, London.

Atkin, B. (1991) New Zealand: Let the family decide – the new approach to family problems. *Journal of Family Law*, 29, No 2, 387–97.

Atkin, B. (1994) New Zealand: 1992 controversy surrounds policies on children. *Journal of Family Law*, 32, No 2, 377–93.

Audit Commission (1994) *Seen But Not Heard – Co-ordinating Community Child Health and Social Services for Children in Need*. HMSO, London.

Audit Commission (1996) *Misspent Youth ... Young People and Crime*. Audit Commission Publications, Abingdon.

Ban, P. & Swain, P. (1994a) Family Group Conferences: Australia's first project within child protection. *Children Australia*, 19, No 3, 19–21.

Ban, P. & Swain, P. (1994b) Family Group Conferences: putting the 'family' back into child protection. *Children Australia*, 19, No 4, 11–14.

Barclay, G.C. (ed) (1995) *Information on the Criminal Justice System in England and Wales, Digest 3*. Home Office Research and Statistics Directorate, London.

Barker, S.O. & Barker, R. (1995) *A Study of the Experiences and Perceptions of 'Family' and 'Staff' Participants in Family Group Conferences (Cwlwm Project)*. MEDRA Research Group, Porthaethwy, Gwynedd.

Bayley, M., Parker, P., Seyd, R. & Tennant, A. (1987) *Practising Community Care – Developing Locally-based Practice*. Joint Unit for Social Services Research at Sheffield University, in collaboration with *Community Care*.

Bebbington, A. & Miles, J. (1989) The background of children who enter local authority care. *British Journal of Social Work*, 19, No 5, 349–68.

Belsky, J. (1980) Child maltreatment: an ecological integration. *American Psychologist*, No 35, 320–35.

Boffa, J. (1995) *The Evaluation of Family Group Conferences – A Key to Family Centered Practice in Child Protection*. Health and Community Services, Melbourne.

Bost, K.K., Cielinsk, K.L., Newell, W.H. & Vaughn, B.E. (1994) Social networks of children attending Head Start from the perspective of the child. *Early Childhood Research Quarterly*, 9, 441–62.

Bott, E. (1957) *Family and Social Network: Roles, Norms and External Relationships in Ordinary Urban Families*. Tavistock Publications, London.

Bott, E. (1971) *Family and Social Network*. Free Press, New York.

Boyce, W.T. (1985) Social support, family relations and children. In: *Social Support and Health* (eds S. Cohert & S. Syme). Academic Press, Orlando, Florida.

Bronfenbrenner, U. (1979) *The Ecology of Human Development*. Harvard University Press, Cambridge, MA.

Bullock, R., Little, M. and Millham, S. (1993) *Going Home – The Return of Children Separated from their Families*. Dartmouth, Aldershot.

Burns, R.B. (1979) *The Self Concept: Theory, Measurement, Development and Behaviour*. Longman, Harlow.

Burnside, J. and Baker, N. (eds) (1994) *Relational Justice: Repairing the Breach*. Waterside Press, Winchester.

Central Statistical Office (1994) *Social Focus on Children*. HMSO, London.

Central Statistical Office (1996) *Social Trends*. HMSO, London.

Cleaver, H. & Freeman, P. (1995) *Parental Perspectives in Cases of Suspected Child Abuse*. HMSO, London.

Cochran, M. & Henderson, C. (1990) Family matters project. In: *Extending Families – The Social Networks of Parents and their Children* (eds M. Cochran, M. Larner, D. Riley *et al.*). Chapter 13. Cambridge University Press, Cambridge.

Cochran, M. & Riley, D. (1990) The social networks of six year olds: context, content and consequence. In: *Extending Families – The Social Networks of Parents and their Children* (eds M. Cochran, M. Larner, D. Riley *et al.*). pp. 154–77. Cambridge University Press, Cambridge.

Cochran, M., Larner, M., Riley, D. *et al.* (eds) (1990) *Extending Families – The Social Networks of Parents and their Children*. Cambridge University Press, Cambridge.

Cockett, M. & Tripp, J. (1994) *The Exeter Family Study*. University of Exeter Press, Exeter.

Cohen, S. & Syme, S. (1985) *Social Support and Health*. Academic Press, Orlando, Florida.

Cohen, S., Mermelstein, R., Karnak, T. & Hoberman, H.M. (1985) Measuring the functional components of social support. In: *Social Support: Theory, Research and Application* (eds I.S. Sarason & L.R. Sarason). pp. 73–94. Martinus Nijhoff, Boston.

Connolly, M. (1994) An Act of empowerment: The Children, Young Persons and their Families Act 1989. *British Journal of Social Work*, 24, No 1, 87–100.

Cotterell, J. (1996) *Social Networks and Social Influences in Adolescence*. Routledge, London.

Cowen, E. (1982) Help is where you find it, *American Psychology*, 37, 385–95.

Cretney, S.M. & Masson, J.M. (1997) *Principles of Family Law*. Sweet and Maxwell, London.

Crockett, L.J. & Crouter, A.C. (eds) (1995) *Pathways Through Adolescence: Individual Development in Relation to Social Contexts*. Erlbaum, Mahwah, NJ.

Crow, G. & Marsh, P. (1997) *Family Group Conferences, Partnership and Child Welfare – A Research Report on Four Pilot Projects in England and Wales*. Partnership Research Programme, University of Sheffield.

Crow, G. & Marsh, P. (in press) *Child Protection, Culture and Family Group Conferences – A Research Report with Haringey Social Service*. Partnership Research Programme, University of Sheffield.

Culbertson, J.L. & Schellenbach, C.J. (1992) Prevention of maltreatment in infants and young children. In: *Prevention of Child Maltreatment: Developmental and Ecological Perspectives* (eds D.J. Willis, E.W. Holden & M. Rosenberg). Wiley & Sons, Chichester.

DeChillo, N., Koren, P.E. & Schultze, K.H. (1994) From paternalism to partnership: family/professional collaboration in children's mental health. *American Journal of Orthopsychiatry*, 64, 564–76.

Dench, G. (1996) *The Place of Men in Changing Family Cultures*. Institute of Community Studies, London.

Department of Health (1995a) *Child Protecvtion – Messages from Research*. HMSO, London.

Department of Health (1995b) *Children and Young People On Child Protection Registers Year Ending 31 March 1995*. Department of Health, London.

Department of Health (1996) *Children Looked after by Local Authorities Year Ending 31 March 1995*. Department of Health, London.

Eckert, P. (1995) Trajectory and forms of institutional participation. In: *Pathways through Adolescence: Individual Development in Relation to Social Contexts* (eds L.J. Crockett & A.C. Crouter). pp. 175–95. Erlbaum, Mahwah, NJ.

Erikson, E. (1963) *Childhood and Society*. Norton, New York.

Farmer, E. & Owen, M. (1995) *Child Protection Practice: Private Risks and Public Remedies*. HMSO, London.

Ferri, E. & Smith, K. (1996) *Parenting in the 1990s*. Family Policy Studies Centre, London.

Finch, J. & Mason, J. (1993) *Negotiating Family Responsibilities*. Routledge, London.

Fisher, M., Marsh, P. & Phillips, D. (1986) *In and Out of Care*. Batsford, London.

Freeman, M.D.A. (1994) Protecting children on both sides of the globe. *Adelaide Law Review*, 16, No 1, 79–98.

Friesen, B.J. & Koroloff, N.M. (1990) Family-centred services: implications for mental health administration and research. *Journal of Mental Health Administration*, 17, No 1, 13–25.

Furman, W. & Buhrmester, D. (1985) Children's perceptions of the personal relationships in their social networks. *Developmental Psychology*, 21, 1016–22.

Gibbons, J. (1990) Family support and prevention: studies in local areas. In:

*DH Yearbook of Research and Development 1990* (eds D. Robbins & A. Walters). HMSO, London.

Gibbons, J. (ed.) (1992) *The Children Act 1989 and Family Support: Principles into Practice.* HMSO, London.

Gibbons, J., Conroy, S. & Bell, C. (1995) *Operating the Child Protection System.* HMSO, London.

Giddens, A. (1991) *Modernity and Self Identity.* Polity Press, Cambridge.

Gilling, M., Patterson, L. & Walker, B. (1995) *Family Members' Experiences of the Care and Protection Family Group Conference Process.* Social Policy Agency, Wellington, New Zealand.

Goffman, E. (1963) *Stigma – Notes on the Management of Spoiled Identity.* Penguin, Harmondsworth.

Graber, L. (1991) *Options Number 26.* Children's Services Department, State of Oregon.

Graber, L., Keys, T. & White, J. (1996) Family group decision-making in the United States: the case of Oregon. In: *Family Group Conferences: perspectives on Policy & Practice* (eds J. Hudson, A. Morris, G.M. Maxwell & B. Galaway), pp. 180–94. The Federation Press, Leichhardt.

Graham, H. (1994) The changing financial circumstances of households with children. *Children and Society*, 8, No 2, 98–113.

Graham, J. & Bowling, B. (1995) *Young People and Crime.* Home Office Research and Planning Unit, Research Study 145, London.

Grimshaw, R. (1996) *Plans and Reviews: Getting it Right for Young People*, National Children's Bureau. To be published in 1997 as *Planning to Care*.

Haimes, E. & Timms, N. (1985) *Adoption, Identity and Social Policy.* Gower, Aldershot.

Hallett, C. (1995) *Interagency Coordination in Child Protection.* HMSO, London.

Hardin, M. (1996) *Family Group Conferences in Child Abuse and Neglect Cases – Learning from the Experience of New Zealand.* American Bar Association Center on Children and the Law, Washington, DC.

Hassall, I.B. (1994) *The Child's Right to a Place – but whose Place? Occasional Paper No 4.* Office of the Commissioner for Children, Wellington, New Zealand.

Hassall, I.B. (1996) Origin and development of Family Group Conferences. In: *Family Group Conferences: Perspectives on Policy & Practice* (eds J. Hudson, A. Morris, G.M. Maxwell & B. Galaway), pp. 17–36. The Federation Press, Leichhardt.

Hassall, I.B. & Maxwell, G.M. (1991) The Family Group Conference. In: *An Appraisal of the First Year of the Children, Young Persons and their Families Act 1989* (ed. I.B. Hassall), pp. 1–13. Office of the Commissioner for Children, Wellington, New Zealand.

Hassall, I.B. & Maxwell, G.M. (1992) *A Children's Rights Approach to Custody and Access – Time for a Radical Rethink.* Office of the Commissioner for Children, Wellington.

Hassall, I.B. & Maxwell, G.M. (1993) *The Impact on Children of Parental Conflict and Divorce*, Conference Paper, Australian Family Research Conference, Sydney.

Henaghan, M. (1992) Questioning the Hassall and Maxwell proposals for custody and access. *Family Law Bulletin*, 3(8), 86–94.

Henaghan, M. & Atkin, B. (1992) *Family Law Policy in New Zealand*. Oxford University Press, Auckland, New Zealand.

Hill, M. (1994) *Family Decision-making in Child Protective Services*. Oregon Children's Services Division, Western Region.

Howe, D. (1992) Child abuse and the bureaucratisation of social work. *The Sociological Review*, 40, No 3, 491–508.

Immarigeon, R. (1996) Family group conferences in Canada and the United States: an overview. In: *Family Group Conferences: Perspectives on Policy & Practice* (eds J. Hudson, A. Morris, G. Maxwell & B. Galaway), pp. 167–79. The Federation Press, Leichhardt.

Jackson, S. & Morris, K. (1994) *Looking at Partnership Teaching in Social Work Qualifying Programmes*. CCETSW, London.

Jordan, B. (1987) Counselling, advocacy and negotiation. *British Journal of Social Work*, 17, 135–46.

Juvenile Justice Drafting Consultancy (1994) *Juvenile Justice for South Africa – Proposals for Legislative and Policy Change*. Institute of Criminology, University of Cape Town, Cape Town.

Kelsey, J. (1995) *The New Zealand Experiment*. Auckland University Press, Auckland.

Kim, U., Triandis, H.C., Kagitcibasi, C. *et al.* (eds) (1994) *Individualism and Collectivism, Theory, Method and Applications*. Sage, London.

Kirchner, P. & Vondraek, S. (1975) Perceived sources of esteem in early childhood. *Journal of Genetic Psychology*, 126, 169–76.

Lagay, B., Campbell, L., Markiewicz, A. *et al.* (1994) *... To Seek the Best Possible Outcomes – An Evaluation of a Pilot Program of Pre-hearing Conferences in the Family Division of the Children's Court of Victoria*. Protective Services Branch of the Victorian Department of Health and Community Services, Melbourne.

Levine, M. & Wyn, H. (1991) *Orders of the Youth Court and the Work of the Youth Justice Co-ordinators*. Evaluation Unit, Department of Social Welfare, Wellington, New Zealand.

Levy, H., Markovic, J., Chaudhry, U. *et al.* (1995) Reabuse rates in a sample of children followed for 5 years after discharge from a child abuse inpatient assessment program, *Child Abuse & Neglect*, 19, No 11, 1363–77.

Longclaws, L., Galaway, B. & Barkwell, L. (1996) Piloting family group conferences for young Aboriginal offenders in Winnipeg, Canada. In: *Family Group Conferences: Perspectives on Policy & Practice* (eds J. Hudson, A. Morris, G. Maxwell & B. Galaway), pp. 195–205. The Federation Press, Leichhardt.

Loughran, G. & Riches, P. (1996) *Working in Partnership with Stepfamilies*. The Learning Agency/National Stepfamily Association, London.

Lupton, C., Barnard, S. & Swall-Yarrington, M. (1995) *Family Planning? An Evaluation of the Family Group Conference Model*. Social Services Research and Information Unit, Portsmouth University, Portsmouth.

Marsh, P. (1990) Changing practice in child care – the Children Act 1989, *Adoption and Fostering*, 14, No 4, 27–30.

Marsh, P. (1991) Child protection case conferences: partnership in practice. In: *Child Protection: A Training and Practice Resource Pack for Work under the Children Act 1989* (eds M. Adcock, R. White & A. Hollows), pp. 35–40. National Children's Bureau, London.

Marsh, P. (1994) Partnership, child protection and family group conferences –
the New Zealand Children, Young Persons and their Families Act 1989.
*Tolley's Journal of Child Law*, 6, No 3, 109–14.

Marsh, P. (1996) The development of FGCs in the UK – an overview. In: *Family
Group Conferences: Messages from UK Practice and Research* (eds K.
Morris & J. Tunnard), pp. 13–20. Family Rights Group, London.

Marsh, P. & Fisher, M. (1992) *Good Intentions: Developing Partnership in
Social Services*. Joseph Rowntree Foundation, York.

Marsh, P. & Triseliotis, J. (eds) (1993) *Prevention and Reunification in Child
Care*. Batsford, London.

Marsh, P. & Crow, G. (1996) Family group conferences in child welfare services in England and Wales. In: *Family Group Conferences: Perspectives on
Policy & Practice* (eds J. Hudson, A. Morris, G. Maxwell & B. Galaway),
pp. 152–66. The Federation Press, Leichhardt.

Marsh, P. & Triseliotis, J. (1996) *Ready to Practise? Social Workers and
Probation Officers: Their Training and First Year in Work*. Avebury,
Aldershot.

Mason, K., Kirby, G. & Wray, R. (1992) *Review of the Children, Young
Persons and their Families Act 1989: Report of the Ministerial Review Team
to the Minister of Social Welfare*. Department of Social Welfare, Wellington,
New Zealand.

Maxwell, G.M. & Morris, A. (1993) *Family, Victims and Culture: Youth
Justice in New Zealand*. Social Policy Agency/Institute of Criminology,
Victoria University, Wellington, New Zealand.

Maxwell, G. & Morris, A. (1996) Research on family group conferences with
young offenders in New Zealand. In: *Family Group Conferences: Perspectives on Policy & Practice* (eds J. Hudson, A. Morris, G. Maxwell & B.
Galaway), pp. 88–110. The Federation Press, Leichhardt.

Maxwell, G., Robertson, J., Thom, A. & Walker, B. (1995) *Researching Care
and Protection*. Office of the Commissioner for Children and Social Policy
Agency/Ropu Here Kaupapa, Wellington, New Zealand.

McGloin, P. & Turnbull, A. (1986) *Parent Participation in Child Abuse Review
Conferences. Planning and Research Section*. London Borough of Green-
wich Social Services Department.

McGlone, F., Park, A. & Roberts, C. (1996) Relative values: kinship and
friendship. In: *British Social Attitudes: The 13th Report* (eds R. Jowell, J.
Curtice, A. Park *et al.*), pp. 53–72. Dartmouth Publishing Company, Aldershot.

Mitchell, A.K. (1985) *Children in the Middle – Living Through Divorce*.
Tavistock, London.

Morgan, J. & Zedner, L. (1992) *Child Victims – Crime, Impact and Criminal
Justice*. Oxford University Press, Oxford.

Moroney, R. (1976) *The Family and the State*. Longman, Harlow.

Morris, K. & Marsh, P. (in press) *Training for Family Group Conferences*.
Family Rights Group, London.

NCH Action for Children (1996) *Factfile 96/7*. NCH Action for Children,
London.

Nestmann, F. & Hurrelmann, K. (1994) *Social Networks and Social Support in
Childhood and Adolescence*. Walter de Gruyter, Berlin.

Newton, C. & Marsh, P. (1993) *Training in Partnership – Translating Intentions into Practice in Social Services*. Joseph Rowntree Foundation, York.

Office for National Statistics (1997) *Social Trends.* The Stationery Office, London.

Orford, J. (1992) *Community Psychology: Theory and Practice.* Wiley & Sons, Chichester.

Packman, J. (1986) *Who Needs Care?* Basil Blackwell, Oxford.

Packman, J. (1993) From prevention to partnership: child welfare services across three decades. *Children & Society,* 7, No 2, 183–95.

Packman, J. & Jordan, B. (1991) The Children Act: looking forward, looking back. *British Journal of Social Work,* 21, No 4, 315–27.

Paolucci, B., Hall, O. & Axinn, N. (1977) *Family Decision Making: An Ecosystem Approach.* John Wiley & Sons, London.

Parke, R.D. & Kellam, S.G. (eds) (1994) *Exploring Family Relationships with other Social Contexts.* Lawrence Erlbaum Associates, New Jersey.

Paterson, J. & Harvey, M. (1991) *An Evaluation of the Organisation and Operation of Care and Protection Family Group Conferences.* Department of Social Welfare, Wellington.

Pennell, J. & Burford, G. (1995a) *Family Group Decision Making: Manual for Coordinators and Communities.* Memorial University of Newfoundland.

Pennell, J. & Burford, G. (1995b) *Family Group Decision Making Project: Implementation Report.* Memorial University of Newfoundland.

Pennell, J. & Burford, G. (1995c) *Family Group Decision Making Project: Implementation Report II.* Memorial University of Newfoundland.

Pennell, J. & Burford, G. (1996) Attending to context: family group decision making in Canada. In: *Family Group Conferences: Perspectives on Policy & Practice* (eds J. Hudson, A. Morris, G. Maxwell & B. Galaway), pp. 206–20. The Federation Press, Leichhardt.

Power, P.J.P. (1996) *Diversionary Conferences: Optimisation and Future Directions,* Conference Paper, Australia and New Zealand Criminology Conference, Wellington, New Zealand.

Pugh, G. & De'Ath, E. (1989) *Working towards Partnership in the Early Years.* National Children's Bureau, London.

Qureshi, H. & Walker, A. (1989) *The Caring Relationship – Elderly People and their Families.* Macmillan, London.

Rai, D.K. (1994) *Developments in Training in Social Services.* National Institute for Social Work, London.

Rautenam, E. (1976) Work with adopted adolescents and adults. In: *Search for Identity,* pp. 32–47. Association of British Agencies for Fostering and Adoption, London.

Renouf, J., Robb, G. & Wells, P. (1990) *Children, Young Persons and their Families Act 1989: Report on First Year of Operation.* Department of Social Welfare, Wellington, New Zealand.

Robertson, J. (1992) How many abused and neglected children? *CHILDREN – A Newsletter from the Office of the Commissioner for Children,* Wellington, New Zealand, 7, 5–6.

Robertson, J. (1996) Research on family group conferences in child welfare in New Zealand. In: *Family Group Conferences: Perspectives on Policy & Practice* (eds J. Hudson, A. Morris, G. Maxwell & B. Galaway), pp. 49–64. The Federation Press, Leichhardt.

Roethlisberger, F.J. & Dickson, W.J. (1939) *Management and the Worker.* Wiley & Sons, Chichester.

Rosen, G. (1994) *A Study of Family Views of Wandsworth's Family Group Conferences*. Wandsworth Social Services, London.

Rutter, M. & Smith, D. (eds) (1995) *Psychosocial Disorders in Young People: Time Trends and their Causes*. Wiley & Sons, Chichester.

Scott, J. & Brook, L. (1997) *Family Change: Demographic and Attitudinal Trends Across Time*. University of Cambridge/Social and Community Planning Research, Economic and Social Research Council, Cambridge.

Shemmings, D. & Thoburn, J. (1990) *Parental Participation in Child Protection Conferences*. University of East Anglia, Norwich.

Shepherd, C. (in press) *The Haringey Family Group Conference Programme*. Partnership Research Programme, University of Sheffield.

Sinclair, I., Crosbie, D. & Vickery, A. (1990) Organisational influences on professional behaviour: factors affecting social work involvement in 'schemes'. *Journal of Social Policy*, 19, No 3, 361–74.

Smale, G., Tuson, G., with Biehal, N. and Marsh, P. (1993) *Empowerment, Assessment, Care Management and the Skilled Worker*. HMSO, London.

Smith, M., Bee, P., Heverin, A. & Nobes, G. (1995) *Parental Control within the Family: The Nature and Extent of Parental Violence to Children*. Thomas Coram Research Unit, Manchester.

Social Services Inspectorate (1991) *Care Management and Assessment – Managers' Guide*. HMSO, London.

Social Services Inspectorate (1995) *The Challenge of Partnership in Child Protection: Practice Guide*. HMSO, London.

Stevenson, O. & Parsloe, P. (1993) *Community Care and Empowerment*. Joseph Rowntree Foundation, York.

Stewart, T. (1996) Family group conferences with young offenders in New Zealand. In: *Family Group Conferences: Perspectives on Policy & Practice* (eds J. Hudson, A. Morris, G. Maxwell & B. Galaway), pp. 65–87. The Federation Press, Leichhardt.

Swain, P. (1993) *Safe in Our Hands – The Evaluation Report of the Family Decision-making Project*. Mission of St James & St John, Melbourne.

Tavecchio, L.W.C. & van IJzendoorn, M.H. (1987) *Attachment in Social Networks*. Elsevier Science, Amsterdam.

Thoburn, J., Lewis, A. & Shemmings, D. (1995) *Paternalism or Partnership? Family Involvement in the Child Protection Process*. HMSO, London.

Thomas, N. (1994) *In the Driving Seat: A Study of the Family Group Meetings Project in Hereford*. Department of Social Policy and Applied Social Studies, University of Wales, Swansea.

Thompson, R.A. (1995) *Preventing Child Maltreatment through Social Support*. Sage, London.

Tunnard, J. (1991a) Setting the scene for partnership. In: *The Children Act 1989: Working in Partnership with Families* (ed. J. Tunnard), pp. 1–6. HMSO, London.

Tunnard, J. (ed.) (1991b) *The Children Act 1989: Working in Partnership with Families*. HMSO, London.

Turner, J. (1978) *Psychosocial Therapy*. Collier Macmillan, London.

Utting, D. (1995) *Family and Parenthood – Supporting Families, Preventing Breakdown*. Joseph Rowntree Foundation, York.

Utting, D. (1996) *Families and Parenting*. Family Policy Studies Centre, London.

Utting, D., Bright, J. & Henricson, C. (1993) *Crime and the Family*. Family Policy Studies Centre, London.

von Dadelszen, J. (1987) *Sexual Abuse Study, An Examination of the Histories of Sexual Abuse among Girls Currently in the Care of the Department of Social Welfare*. Research Section, Department of Social Welfare, Wellington, New Zealand.

Walgrave, L. (1995) Restorative justice for juveniles: just a technique or a fully fledged alternative? *The Howard Journal*, 34, No 3, 228–49.

Wellington District Family Law Committee (1992) Response to the Hassall–Maxwell paper. *Family Law Bulletin*, 3(10), 114–18.

Wenger, G.C. (1984) *The Supportive Network*. George Allen and Unwin, London.

Wenger, G.C. (1994) *Understanding Support Networks and Community Care: Network Assessment For Elderly People*. Avebury, Aldershot.

Wundersitz, J. & Hetzel, S. (1996) Family conferencing for young offender: the South Australian experience. In: *Family Group Conferences: Perspectives on Policy & Practice* (eds J. Hudson, A. Morris, G. Maxwell & B. Galaway), pp. 111–39. The Federation Press, Leichhardt.

Younghusband, E. (1978) *Social Work in Britain: 1950–1975 Vol 1*. George Allen and Unwin, London.

# Index